THE STORYTELLING COACH

Several of the coaching sessions described in this book are available on an instructional videotape:

Coaching Storytellers: A Demonstration Workshop for All Who use oral Communication. (Enchanters Press, P.O. Box 441195, West Sommerville, MA 02144, 617-391-3672).

THE STORYTELLING COACH

How to Listen, Praise, and Bring Out People's Best

DOUG LIPMAN

August House Publishers, Inc.
LITTLE ROCK

Published 1995 by August House, Inc.,
P.O. Box 3223, Little Rock, Arkansas, 72203,
501-372-5450.

Printed in the United States of America

10 9 8 7 6 5 4 3 2 1 HB
10 9 8 7 6 5 4 3 2 PB

LIBRARY OF CONGRESS CATALOGING-IN-PUBLICATION DATA
Lipman, Doug.
The storytelling coach: how to listen, praise,
and bring out people's best/ Doug Lipman.
p. cm.
ISBN 0-87483-435-X (alk. paper).—ISBN 0-87483-434-1 (pb: alk. paper)
1. Storytelling-Study and teaching. I. Title.
LB1042.L52 1995
372.64'2044—dc20 95-32696P

Executive editor: Liz Parkhurst
Project editor: Rufus Griscom
Design director: Ted Parkhurst
Cover design: Harvill Ross Studios Ltd.

The paper used in this publication meets the minimum requirements of
the American National Standard for Information Sciences—Permanence of
Paper for Printed Library Materials, ANSI Z39.48-1984.

AUGUST HOUSE, INC. PUBLISHERS LITTLE ROCK

"If I have seen further ...
it is by standing upon the shoulders of Giants."
—Sir Isaac Newton

To my father.
Too short to play football.
Among teachers, a giant.

CONTENTS

ACKNOWLEDGMENTS

Each teacher who has taught me well has added to my knowledge of what is possible in teaching—and of how to achieve it. My parents, my grandmother, and my cousin Roger taught me well again and again. My brother Brad thought I could do anything; as a result, I often did more than I would have thought possible.

I remember Freddie Werdebaugh acting as though a seven-year-old could learn to whistle—and so I did.

I remember a string of delighted grade-school teachers, especially Mr. Saline, the gym teacher—who structured our activities in a way that showed his expectations and allowed us to notice our own progress.

In high school, Richard Gragg had the unusual attitude that literature was more about having fun than about being right. Others whose words and attitudes are still with me include Tom MacMahon, John Handzel, Gerald Boevers, and Edward Brufke.

Elliot Coleman was the first to believe in me more than I did. George Garrett, Richard Dillard, John Moore and others at Hollins College knew that nurture was as important as challenge.

Lisa Parker was the first music teacher to believe in me; therefore, she changed my life. Frances Aronoff, Lillian Yaross, and Chris Krueger each helped me discover more of what was possible for me—in spite of my lurking suspicions that I could not succeed.

My months at the Kodály Musical Training Institute were filled with the joy of being surrounded by excellent teachers who took it as their responsibility that I would learn. My debt is especially great to Kati Komlos, Klara Nemes, Lenci Horvath, and

Janos Horvath.

Debby Saperstone introduced me to Re-Evaluation Counseling, thus adding greatly to my tools for teaching. Many teachers of co-counseling helped me over the years, especially Alan Epstein, Anamika Neitlich, and Lisa Wanzor.

Two of my supervisors in preschool teaching taught me the value and mechanics of praise: Sally Braun and Edra Mercer.

Numerous storytelling students and colleagues became my first "rehearsal buddies," thus helping me learn the great strength of artistic partnerships. I think first of Melissa Silva, Lee-Ellen Marvin, Don Futterman, Jennifer Justice, Judith Black, Elisa Pearmain, Derek Burrows, and Jay O'Callahan, among many others.

The thinking behind this book emerged during helpful conversations and good coaching from my four mainstays, Linda Palmström, Jay O'Callahan, Marsha Saxton, and Christine Shumock. The actual writing was accomplished in the company of my writing buddies, including Marsha Saxton, Jay O'Callahan, Lyn Hoopes, Linda Langford, Terry Marrotta and Patricia McCallum. If every Boston-area writer knew of the hospitality and good humor of Michael, Michael, and Jeff, there would never be any seats empty in the Brookline Deli. How many restaurants do you know where the single-line phone rings, and the owner says to a customer, "It's for you—on line one!"

These people gave crucial help with the manuscript: Wanna Zinsmaster, Linda Borodkin, Lisa Wanzor, Jay O'Callahan, and Carrie van der Laan.

To all the people I have coached, I quote the Talmud:

As much as the calf wishes to suck, even more does the cow wish to give suck. By this we mean: as much as the student wishes to learn, even more does the teacher wish to teach.

Thank you all for allowing me to coach you.

My strongest and closest partner has been Linda Palmström, my wife. She is my great ally in all things large and little, sweet and salty, fundamental and funny. I would not be so brave a coach without her.

Foreword

In the last seven years, Doug Lipman has been part of every story I've worked on. Our coaching sessions themselves have become stories.

* * *

Last year, Doug Lipman and I were in a recording studio at WGBH public radio station in Boston. I was recording a difficult and fascinating story called "Father Joe." The story is complicated because it is both a celebration of my uncle's heroism on board an aircraft carrier during WWII, and a portrayal of our relationship during my college days. The whole idea of the story is to show that my uncle was a teacher in the deepest sense.

The story is an hour long and it was a challenge to record it as well as I wanted. I was alone in the studio and two friends were in the recording booth. I couldn't see them, but evidently they were cheering because twenty minutes of the story went well. When I got to the battle, the scenes just weren't working. I was describing a raging fire on board my uncle's ship. I just couldn't seem to do it properly.

Doug came into the studio, gave me a hug and said, "You're doing great. The first twenty minutes of the story is perfect. How do you feel?"

"Breathless. And worried."

"Worried about what?"

"I'm headed down to Chile in a week. If I don't get it right now I'll have to wait six months." Doug smiled and said, "If I thought you should wait, I'd say so. You're ready. What do you mean breathless?"

"The moment the ship is hit the story roars away from me. I can't find the rhythms. I feel out of control. I can't find the rhythms ... the pacing."

Doug said, "Tell a bit of the story and I'll stay here and dance the emotions." So I told the fiery scene while Doug stood in front of me, and eyes shut, he moved to the emotions of the scene. It calmed me down and I was able to do it properly. For the next thirty or forty minutes as I told the story, Doug, eyes shut, was doing a kind of Shiva dance. It was an extraordinary moment. It revealed so much about Doug. His dance was an act of creativity, friendship, and great generosity. Doug had never done anything like this before, and may never do anything like it again. But I was stuck, and the moment called for something very special. Doug listened and discovered what that something special was.

So here in this single moment, we had many of the crucial elements of coaching. Doug listened intently, and appreciated what I was doing. At the same time, he realized I wasn't doing my best. He asked me several questions, and in the questioning discovered what I needed.

In a sense, what Doug did was startling, and it contradicted what I'd been taught, i.e., concentrate on what's wrong. Doug could have come down to the studio and said, "You're overdramatizing. Just calm it down." Or he could have said, "We're running out of time, maybe we should try it when you come back from Chile." Instead, it was clear he was fully committed to me, and to the story, and to the success of doing the recording right then. He sensed there was no reason to put it off.

That's just one example of the many times that Doug Lipman has been an invaluable friend and coach. We live in a world where we expect that we can do everything for ourselves. Of course we can't, and we often feel isolated. Doug has discovered that one way through isolation is just to find someone to listen to us. And after listening, someone can appreciate what we do. This seems simple and it is. At the same time it contradicts a whole mythology. It contradicts the mythology of the lone cowboy who solves everything all by himself. It contradicts the idea of the tubercular artist wasting away in the attic. It contradicts the view of the artist as a sourpuss, as an isolated grump who scowls and turns out masterpieces. These myths have their charm, but they're both absurd and destructive. Doug's book is invaluable because it gives us another vision. It gives us a vision of the artistic relationship. Along with Walt Whitman, I believe we are all artists. *The Storytelling Coach* gives us a vision of encouraging creativity by listening, supporting, and appreciating.

* * *

One of the most challenging and difficult stories I've ever done is called "The Dance." "The Dance" explores the teenage years. I never thought I would do a story about the high school years because it was a hard time. But I began the story, and I felt a great force. Perhaps Doug's greatest contribution during this time was to say, "I'm so proud of you for taking this on, Jay." It's so important to have at least one person in the world to say, "Good for you to take this on." That became the mantra. I knew Doug believed it, and that support was invaluable.

* * *

Recently my daughter, Laura, was illustrating a children's book of mine. Laura reached a point where she felt alone and stuck. I described the problem to Doug over breakfast, and as usual he listened. He listened well enough to realize this was very important to me. When we got back to my office, Doug phoned Laura and asked what she needed to go on with her work. "I'm stuck," Laura said. "I feel paralyzed." Doug listened patiently and asked again, "What do you need to feel unstuck?"

"Well ..." Laura began. Doug's repeated question allowed Laura to concentrate not on being paralyzed but on what she needed to go on with her work. Laura's answer poured out, "I need the publisher to say she still believes in my work." I volunteered to call the publisher and relay Laura's message. The publisher listened to me and immediately phoned Laura and reassured her. Laura felt relieved and empowered. She finished the illustrations. Beautifully.

This is an example of how Doug visualizes people—Laura in this case, feeling free, confident, and creative. Doug asked his question with that image of Laura in mind.

There are times in anyone's life when the choices are difficult. Several years ago, the Boston Symphony Orchestra asked me to compose a story that I would tell with the orchestra. I met with people from the Boston Symphony Hall, and it was all very exciting. Right after that meeting, I flew to St. Louis for the National Storytelling Conference. I realized on the way that it would be best to turn the Boston Symphony Orchestra down because I very much wanted to use the summer to create a story about growing up. I felt the story needed those months to burst through. So I called the Boston Symphony and said no. They called back and said yes. They said, "You really ought to do this. You'd have a wonderful time and we need you to do this." Well, how do you say "no" to that? How often in life does the Boston Symphony Orchestra tell you they need you? This was for the family concert series; it wasn't the absolute mountaintop, but it was pretty far up the hill. Fortunately, Doug Lipman and I flew home together and were able to talk the problem over. What Doug did was listen. As Doug listened and I talked, it became clearer to me that my need to create the story of youth was very great indeed. It had been growing inside for a lifetime, and now it was time. I asked for Doug's thoughts and he had listened carefully enough to appreciate my need to create a new story. It was Doug's listening and appreciation that allowed me to call the Boston Symphony one final time and say I couldn't do the program at that time. A new story, "Chickie," was born. It allowed me to go on as an artist.

Doug Lipman teaches us that the good coach puts the coachee first. Conventional wisdom would have said I mustn't turn down the BSO. Doug saw in this case there was a deeper priority!

Reading this book helps us become much better listeners. And if we're better listeners, we can be better parents, teachers, and artists; we can be better people.

* * *

Several years ago, my son, Ted, and I decided to hike the Appalachian Trail for three weeks down in North Carolina and Tennessee. We chose the most difficult part of the whole Appalachian Trail. I had not done any mountain climbing, and I knew this was going to be difficult. Ted and I were going to be carrying packs that weighed forty or fifty pounds. And we were leaving the world and hiking in this great mountain range.

Doug and I talked the trip over at breakfast one morning before our usual coaching session. Doug listened to my worries about the trip, and he said, "Do you want a suggestion?" Doug always asks if I want a suggestion. That's very helpful because sometimes I don't. Sometimes I just want a listener. In this case, I said yes, and Doug said, "Just remember this, there's at least one elegant solution to every problem."

That simple sentence was very freeing and it came back to Ted and me time after time on the trail. I remember one morning we were exhausted because of the extremely difficult climb the day before. I came to a stream and was furious when I saw an empty can that had been thrown into the stream. Just then, another camper came along behind me and wanted to fill his water bottle up. He stooped down and picked up the can, and he crushed it and turned it into a funnel. Using the can as a funnel, he filled his water bottle. I too, having no funnel, filled my water bottle with the newly made spout. I smiled and thought of Doug saying, "There's at least one elegant solution to every problem." Doug himself finds elegant solutions all the time. The good news is with this book, he's teaching us to do the same.

* * *

When I think about Doug's book, I think of drama coaches, storytellers, teachers, parents, actors, artists, and businesspeople reading the book and thinking more carefully about the power of listening. And then I think of them learning through this book how to appreciate and how to bring out people's best. I think of people reading this book and saying, "Oh, I thought criticism meant telling people what's wrong. I had no idea listening could be creative and that appreciating what one has done well could be freeing and empowering."

We all want to be creative in life. We want to be creative in our work, in our play, in our ordinary life. We need an approach that liberates, welcomes, and frees our creativity. That's what this book is about.

There is no question that Doug Lipman is a greatly gifted coach, but more important is the fact that he realizes others can be fine coaches. Doug has a powerful sense of structure, and he's thought out coaching in a way no one else has. I'm very proud of him for doing this book. This book is a great gift to the storytelling community. It's a great gift to teachers and people in the helping professions, to actors, parents ... all of us. It's full of clear thinking, humor, wonderful examples, and underlying it all is Doug's awareness that good coaching can bring out the beauty and the power of every human being.

Jay O'Callahan
Marshfield, Massachusetts

Introduction

Suddenly, coaches are everywhere. People who once might have called themselves "consultant," "tutors," or just plain "teachers" are giving their role a new name.

Why? It seems that many of us are dissatisfied with how we have been given help—whether we have been helped with our presentations, our learning of something new, our managerial style, or our creative output. Something about the word "coach" holds the promise of a new, supportive, yet meaningful style of assistance.

This book defines a new way of coaching, which is effective because it is based on respect for you—the person being helped—and for your abilities. This form of coaching aims to enlist your imagination and intelligence, not to have your helper do the thinking for you. It starts from a belief in your unique abilities and goes on to identify and help you overcome each obstacle to your success.

For me, the helper, to learn this new way of coaching, I must sometimes depart from my automatic responses, which I have internalized from my experiences of being taught and instructed over the years. To make such a departure possible, this book gives both the principles to be followed by this new kind of coach and many detailed examples of coaching in action.

The examples are all drawn from my years as a coach of storytellers. The applications, however, extend to nearly every helping relationship. If you are a helper in any field, or wish to be a better informed consumer of help, read on.

You are about to meet a new kind of helper, the Storytelling Coach.

Learning to Help Storytellers

In the spring of 1979, I attended the first public "story sharing" group in the Boston area.

A storyteller stood up and told a story. Poorly.

I thought, "I'm very glad this is not happening in my storytelling class. If it were, I would be expected to help this person improve. And I have no idea how to help him." Cringing, I said nothing.

Many years later, having helped hundreds of storytellers and other oral communicators, I was leading a coaching workshop.

A storyteller stood up and told a story.

Not perfectly, but quite well.

I thought, "I'm not sure how to help this person get even better."

For a moment, I felt the old fear: I'm supposed to know how to help, but I don't.

Then I remembered that, among the many things I have learned about coaching over the years, I have learned not to pretend.

I said confidently, "I don't have any suggestions to make."

The storyteller said, "Thank you. That's the best thing you could have said to me."

This book contains what I learned between those two moments, and how it relates to helping relationships of many kinds. This introduction tells how I learned it, and why.

It was the fall of 1978. The final session of my course for day care teachers, "Meeting the Needs of Young Children Through Music," had just ended. One of my students, Bobbie London, was telling me how much she had enjoyed the course. I thanked her for her praise.

"I liked your course in early childhood curriculum, too."

I thanked Bobbie again.

"And I only have one course to go before I can get a certificate."

I congratulated her.

"And you're the only teacher in the college who I like."

Trying vainly to be humble, I thanked her again.

"No, Doug, you don't understand. I want you to come up with another course to teach so that I can take it."

Frantically, I tried to think of what to say. Bobbie's suggestion was flattering, but disconcerting. I was only an adjunct faculty member in the evening division of a junior college. I didn't have any control over curriculum, or any reason to believe that the college wanted any more courses.

Besides, what else could I teach? I was a half-time nursery school teacher and a free-lance musician. I taught teachers how to play guitar and lead musical activities with children. I had only taught the curriculum course because the regular professor was away for a semester and they needed a teacher on short notice.

Just a month earlier, I had tried unsuccessfully to establish myself as a school music performer. I had called my former supervisor, the head of the music department in an elementary school district. He told me that he liked my work but had a huge surplus of folk musicians just then. Then he said, "Doug, sometimes you include stories with your songs. Across the hall in the Literary Resources Department, they are looking for storytellers. Call them." For the first time, I had heard the label of "storyteller." Up until that moment, I had thought of storytelling as a branch of music.

I thought, that's it! I said to Bobbie, "I also do storytelling. Would you want a course in that?"

"That's a great idea. Bruno Bettelheim's new book is about storytelling. It's a perfect subject for day care teachers. Teach it next semester so I can finish my certificate."

AFTER THE FIRST STUDENT'S STORY

When I proposed the new course, I was told that storytelling was not a big enough subject for a whole course—but, if I wanted, I could cover it as part of a course in Children's Literature.

The next spring, I found myself facing a new class of adult students. I began the course by saying, "This is Children's Literature and Storytelling. The only children's literature we cover will be oral children's literature. I hope no one is disappointed."

I knew nothing about teaching storytelling, of course. Others were teaching courses in the art of storytelling, but to my knowledge—with the exception of some library schools and in traditional cultures—there was virtually no living tradition of teaching storytelling.

One activity that seemed obvious was for the students to tell stories to each other. Over the next weeks, I explained, each student would have a turn to tell a story in front of the entire class.

Once the first student told her story, however, she seemed to want a response from me. What should I say?

HOW MY FATHER TAUGHT ME

If I had been raised differently, I might have assumed that my job was to tell the student storyteller what she had done wrong.

But I was my father's son.

From the time I was born, my father showed delight in my learning. He took each success of mine as a further confirmation of his expectation that I was a smart child.

When I was just learning to speak, he spent hours carrying me around our studio apartment, pointing to objects, saying their names, then waiting for me to imitate what he said. When I said, "Door," he repeated gleefully, "Door! He said, 'Door'!" When I mispronounced a word, he was just as gleeful. "A-pull. He called an apple 'a-pull'!"

As I grew, he made himself available to answer my questions about the world. He explained photography, car engines, and how to write poetry. In every case, he expected me to succeed and even to go beyond his own level of understanding. He delighted in my triumphs and lent me a hand when I failed.

For years, my father's teaching seemed to have no connection to "teaching" as I experienced it in school. Like children of immigrant or otherwise "different" parents, I compartmentalized my experience, maintaining different sets of expectations for my father-teacher and my school-teachers.

When I went away to college, for the first time I lacked the support of my father's teaching. Not knowing what was missing, I felt an indefinite yearning. When I chanced upon a teacher who began by expecting me to succeed (see "Elliot Coleman's Gift," page 55), I latched onto his methods and even his subject matter. I changed my career plans to postpone graduate work in mathematics so I could spend a year studying creative writing. As it turned out, once I had experienced other great writing teachers (see the second half of "The Famous Story I Will Never Read," page 68), I never returned to mathematics.

LEARNING TO COACH

As I faced the student who had just told her story to the class, I sensed her desire for a response.

I had two models of teaching, that of my father and that of the majority of my schoolteachers. In a dim way, I knew that I wanted to respond to my student storyteller as my father would have.

But how had my father responded to me? He had never talked about the principles of teaching. None of the other good teachers I had found had spoken of their methods. How could I adapt their approach to helping storytellers?

Through trial and error, I began what I later decided to call "coaching." My only guides were my internal sense of the best teaching I had received, and the look on my students' faces as I met—or failed to meet—their unspoken expectations.

Bumbling along, I gradually discovered the value of telling storytellers what they were doing well. After several disasters in which I substituted my goals for those of the storyteller, I learned the value of respecting the teller's goals.

Over the next years, I continued teaching storytelling and continued trying to learn to teach it. I learned from experiences in many realms, whether in classes, board meetings, or computer user groups. Whenever I attended any kind of event where people seemed to learn easily, I tried to understand what techniques had led to success.

When I applied techniques that worked, I saw joy on my students' faces.

One year I offered a workshop on coaching at Sharing the Fire, the regional storytelling conference in New England. For a handout, I prepared my first list of "coaching principles." Over the years, I have continued to reformulate that list, culminating in the principles given here in the "Coaching Principles" chapter.

Building on structures employed in counseling and other fields, I slowly developed the four-part structure for a coaching session, described in the "A Structure for Coaching" chapter.

Since the ideas of coaching are not only ancient and obvious but also startling and uncommon these days, I have tried to reinforce them with stories throughout the text. In the appendix on "Sources" I give my sources for the stories as well as the background facts for the various edited coaching sessions throughout the book.

The Need and the Opportunity

After several years of teaching storytelling, I realized the unique situation faced by the storytelling revival.

In the 1960s and 1970s, people around the world began to discover storytelling. Again and again, people who happened to tell a story to a group of children noticed the children's intense interest and hunger for more. Others who told to adults, to elders, or to family groups realized the appeal and benefit of this ancient form of communication. Each time, they made an independent discovery of the value of storytelling in the modern age.

Only in 1973, with the first National Storytelling Festival in

Tennessee, did this spontaneous storytelling movement gain a focus. Year after year, people learned about the Festival and said, "Storytelling? Why, that's what I've been doing. I thought I was the only one! I'll have to meet those other storytellers."

The Need for Helpers

Of course, many of these storytellers began to hunger for helpers.

In other art forms, there are time-honored methods for improving. Graphic artists get critiqued, actors get directed, musicians take individual lessons, and performing artists of all stripes attend schools to improve their art.

But in storytelling, no such traditional approach exists. In the mainstream culture of the United States, storytellers have an individual art form with no apprenticeships, no certification, no recognized course of study. If a great actor decides she wants help with her acting, she knows she can go to a director or an acting coach. If a storyteller at any level wants help, he doesn't even know a term that describes the person he seeks.

If we're going to help each other, we'll have to create a way to do it.

Of course, our situation is not really unique. Other fields have no established helping tradition. Still others have traditions that badly need restructuring or alternative forms.

The Opportunity to Start Fresh

Along with our almost complete lack of established forms of help, we storytellers have a unique opportunity to create our own tradition. Actors, musicians, and graphic artists are certainly helped by their directors and teachers, but they are also hindered by ineffective practices that have sometimes become institutionalized.

Storytellers don't have that problem.

Since we are starting from scratch, we can create a new tradition of help that is based, from the beginning, on the most effective methods currently available.

We can use our interest in storytelling to form coaching relationships (discussed on pages 223-237) that have the same qualities of sharing, hopefulness, and respect that we value in storytelling itself.

Others can learn from the efforts of storytellers to create a fresh, effective tradition of helping.

What to Call Our Helpers

Since we don't have a name for the person who helps a storyteller, I propose the term "coach."

In sports, a coach can only succeed when the whole team succeeds.

A "critic" might prefer being right to being helpful, but a coach is focused on a goal of achievement.

A "director" might be the one to set the artistic goals, but a coach supports an athlete to achieve her own goals. If the director is like a co-parent to the story, the coach is like a midwife.

A "teacher" might be thought to impart a fixed body of knowledge, but a coach helps the athlete exceed the coach's abilities. A storytelling coach assists the storyteller in fulfilling his own uniqueness.

The term "coach," therefore, can remind us of some of the basic principles of supportive, respectful helping.

Not Just for Storytellers

The more I tell others what we storytellers are learning about coaching, the more they claim it for themselves, too.

Artists of all kinds have embraced this model of coaching, but they are by no means alone.

A storyteller carried a draft of this book home. Two weeks later, she said, "My husband has already incorporated your ideas into the saxophone lessons he gives. And my son's soccer coach has changed the way he structures soccer practice."

A small-business owner heard me talk about the principles of coaching. The next week, facing a difficult meeting with his employees, he tried applying the principles to his interactions with his workers. By the end of that day-long meeting, a new creativity had been unleashed. Ending months of impasse, the owner and his employees created a new image for their enterprise.

Others from various fields have taken these principles to heart, whether they are writers, organizational development consultants, editors, educators, or computer software developers.

Even though the ideas in this book apply to many fields, the examples are taken from storytelling, the field I know best. But please don't be put off by the frequent mention of storytelling. I believe that these examples have broad relevance, for two reasons.

First, in the broad sense, "story" is part of most oral communication. You will use narrative when you defend a business proposal, explain your objections to an inconsiderate neighbor, or set forth your vision of a new world order.

Second, the principles and structures of coaching storytellers are adaptable for any field—your field, in particular. In this book, one chapter describes detailed hints for adapting these principles for the classroom. Using the principles, the detailed examples from the field of storytelling, and this sample adaptation, you should be able to apply these methods to any situation you encounter.

To make it clear that coaching is helpful for working on more than just stories, I refer briefly to other kinds of projects or productions, or just use the generic terms "presentation" or "project."

NOT THE LAST WORD

Since coaching as I describe it is still a new art, it will continue to change.

There is no cookbook for coaching, but there are principles, guidelines, and points to consider. Our ability to describe these factors will continue to improve. Therefore, I expect the formulations in this book to be superseded—the sooner, the better.

Individual moments of good coaching, on the other hand—

like my father's moments of teaching me well—are never completely obsolete. Therefore, I have included many coaching examples which demonstrate helping storytellers to overcome specific obstacles.

Imagine the state of storytelling coaching—or of helping relationships in general—a hundred years from now. If some interested would-be coach comes across this book, what will she say?

If she says, "This is clearly the best book on coaching ever written," then I will have failed. You and others like you will not have used the contents of this book to take the art of coaching to a higher level.

But if she says, "This book has some good moments, but is unbelievably primitive by current coaching standards," then I will have succeeded.

We will all have made this book into the first word of a long, exciting story.

COACHING PRINCIPLES

Why coaching? Why not critiquing, instructing, directing, or evaluating?

Because the word "coaching" reminds us that the coach succeeds only when the team succeeds.

As your coach, my success depends entirely on yours. Every thing I do as an effective coach is calculated to contribute to your success.

Coaching is supportive and cooperative. We work together to create success for both of us.

Believe in Success

If you can't succeed, then I can't succeed as your coach either.

Therefore, to accept the job of coaching you, I need to believe in the possibility of your success.

Believing in your success can mean one of two things.

Some believe there is only one way to succeed. For them, success means being the best, going to the Olympics, winning the Nobel Prize, or becoming the CEO. In other words, success means capturing something that is scarce, that not everyone can have.

Others believe there are many ways to succeed. They believe it is not better to be Picasso than to be Rembrandt, to be Mozart rather than Beethoven.

In this second view, we each have something unique to offer.

To develop it, to offer it clearly, fully, and powerfully—is to succeed. Beethoven did not fail to become another Mozart; he succeeded at becoming Beethoven. Seen this way, success comes from developing your uniqueness. It is rare but not scarce. Every one, potentially, can succeed.

In some endeavors, the belief in a single form of success may make sense. Professional sports, for example, hold our attention over a defined time period because we agree to focus on some narrow objective: getting the ball through the hoop more times, or being the first in a line of skaters.

In most areas of life, however, it makes more sense to believe in the diversity of success.

Art, learning, spirituality, and family life—to choose just a few examples—are all complex endeavors. They are interesting precisely because the focus is broad. There is no single goal. There are many ways to "win" at life. (Even in sports, we can choose to measure success by multiple goals, including enjoyment or progress.)

The coach who defines success as winning the Olympics must choose athletes carefully, since only a few have such potential. But the coach of students, of storytellers, of artists, of athletes who value something more than winning, can freely take on anyone willing to try.

We can all be coached, because we all have the ability to succeed.

When I, as your coach, treat you as though I expect you to succeed, you are actually more likely to succeed. When you do succeed, I am more likely to continue to expect you to succeed. My belief in your success carries within it the seed of an upward spiral.

THE DIVERSITY OF SUCCESS

In the case of storytellers, the diversity of success is especially easy to notice.

Let us suppose, for example, that each of three excellent

storytellers tells a version of the same folktale, such as "Cinderella." One tells it with deep pathos, leading us to cry at Cinderella's trials and rage at her abusers. Another tells it with quiet confidence, leading us to hope for Cinderella's survival and to cheer at her triumph. A third tells it with humor, mocking the conventions of the fairytale itself, leading us to laugh at our own expectations.

To be sure, any particular listener may prefer one of these three performances over the others. After all, some prefer Mozart over Beethoven. Just as Mozart and Beethoven both succeeded as composers, however, all three storytellers have succeeded artistically.

Most human endeavors resemble storytelling more than they resemble the Olympics. Artists of all kinds, parents, teachers, administrators, therapists, organizational development consultants, and politicians all can succeed in unique ways.

✧ Zusia ✧

Once, the great Hasidic leader, Zusia, came to his followers. His eyes were red with tears, and his face was pale with fear.

"Zusia, what's the matter? You look frightened!"

"The other day, I had a vision. In it, I learned the question that the angels will one day ask me about my life."

The followers were puzzled. "Zusia, you are pious. You are scholarly and humble. You have helped so many of us. What question about your life could be so terrifying that you would be frightened to answer it?"

Zusia turned his gaze to heaven. "I have learned that the angels will not ask me, 'Why weren't you a Moses, leading your people out of slavery?' "

His followers persisted. "So, what will they ask you?"

"And I have learned," Zusia sighed, "that the angels will not ask me, 'Why weren't you a Joshua, leading your people into the promised land?' "

One of his followers approached Zusia and faced him squarely. Looking him in the eyes, the follower demanded, "But what will they ask you?"

"They will say to me, 'Zusia, there was only one thing that no power of heaven or earth could have prevented you from becoming.' They will say, 'Zusia, why weren't you Zusia?' "

NO MORE MR. RIGHT

Believing in the diversity of success flies directly in the face of an attitude that seemed to underlie many of the literature classes I attended from high school to graduate school. This unspoken assumption might be phrased: there is only one correct meaning of a piece of literature, and our job is to determine it.

A more helpful attitude for the coach might be phrased like this: there are an infinite number of interpretations of each story, and my job is to help the storyteller discover her unique interpretation and present it beautifully.

More generally, the coach's attitude is that there are an infinite number of ways to accomplish any task in a meaningful way.

The coach's job is not to be right, but to be helpful.

IF THERE'S NO RIGHT WAY, WHICH WAY DO WE GO?

If many kinds of success are possible, which kind of success should I help you pursue? How can the coach know whether a particular storyteller will succeed better through pathos or through humor? How do I know whether an administrator will lead best through visible leadership or behind-the-scenes encouragement?

Fortunately, the coach is not primarily responsible for this decision. In most cases, it is not my decision at all; it is yours.

Honor the Goals

The successful coach helps you achieve your goals, not the coach's goals.

If you come to me with eight of your friends and say, "We want you to coach our baseball team," you would expect me to help you achieve your goal of playing baseball.

You would be shocked if I rented skates and sticks for you and scheduled a hockey practice. If I said, "I don't like baseball. You're going to play hockey!" you would probably hire yourself another coach.

Unfortunately, some would-be coaches may not frame the issue so clearly. They may muddy the waters by adding ridicule or bribery, to coerce you to accept their goal. They might say: "Baseball is stupid. Hockey is the intelligent, classy game, preferred by the superior person." Or: "You don't have a chance as ball players. But I happen to know of an opening in a hockey league. Your team could be a contender!" (This last might be an appropriate suggestion, by the way, if your goal was "to play a team sport in a league," but it does not further your goal of playing baseball.)

WHY CAN'T I ACCEPT YOUR GOALS?

Why isn't it obvious to the coach that the goals pursued by a helper should be those of the person being helped? Why would anyone accept or offer help that ignores or subverts the goals of the person seeking help?

Most of us, as children, have had our ability to set goals undermined by adults who arrogated the role of goal-setting. Over years, we were consistently deprived of simple respect. We were not asked what we wanted to learn. Then we were not helped to achieve our goals in a unique way.

If I was thus distrusted to set my own goals, I may not have fully developed my ability to set goals. I may not find it easy to trust you to set your own goals, either.

I may have even been forced to choose between two undesirable alternatives: going without help or having my goals preempted. Choosing the first alternative left me isolated; choosing the second, powerless. If these were the only two choices available to me, I may have not yet grasped the possibility of helping relationships that are both connected and empowering.

HELPING THROUGH HONORING

If people may not have fully developed their abilities to set goals, one might ask, doesn't that make it unwise to defer to their goals?

There are at least three reasons to honor the goals of those being coached, even if their goals may not be fully appropriate or sensible at the moment.

First, honoring their goals empowers the people being helped. People learn most efficiently when they control the learning process.

To illustrate this idea, I have only to remember my days as a teacher of folk guitar to children. When I dragged children through a pre-set curriculum of songs and strums, most of them were slowed by each increase in difficulty, no matter how slight. It might take months for them to learn a new right-hand strumming pattern. One day, however, a child convinced me to let her try playing a song that she loved, even though it came months later in the curriculum. To my amazement, she learned it—and its advanced right-hand pattern—perfectly in only two weeks. After that, I tried to help each child find favorite songs. They continued to astonish me by learning things that were "too difficult" for them! When they set the goals, they learned many times faster than when I set the goals.

Second, you know more than I do about your needs, desires, and difficulties. What is helpful for you depends not only on the part of your life that is visible to me, but also on the part that is hidden. For example, you may need the satisfaction of an easy triumph one day and the stimulation of a great challenge another. As coach, I cannot possibly have complete access to your huge mental database; you are the world's greatest expert about yourself.

Third, if you haven't yet learned to set goals, you need practice at goal-setting. You won't gain skill at it if I always set goals for you.

Pursuing the "wrong" goal can actually help you learn to set goals better. After achieving the goal you thought you wanted, for example, you will be in an unparalleled position to discover that the goal was not, in fact, the one you really wanted. Until then, your learning about goal-setting may be suspended, frozen in the belief that you know the appropriate goal but have not yet gotten the help you need to attain it.

Thus, by honoring your goals, I give you indirect help in setting better ones. Of course, I can also give you direct help with goal-setting by helping you discover what a story (or other presentation or project) means to you, and your intentions in telling it. (See "Needing More Experience of the Story," pages 111-135.)

Letting you set your own goals is a powerful tool for helping you succeed. After all, your success (in a complex activity like storytelling or community organizing) depends on developing your unique combination of abilities, so that you can communicate your unique point of view. Pursuing your particular goals is an integral part of your uniqueness, and therefore of your success.

WHAT ABOUT MY JUDGMENT?

If the goals we pursue together are yours, is my judgment useless to you? Must I hold back from every comment or judgment for fear I am treading on your uniqueness?

Of course not. There are many situations in which my judgment as coach can be invaluable.

Above all, there is one use of my critical faculties that is reliably helpful in a wide range of situations: giving praise.

Give Praise

In our society, we often seem squeamish about giving praise. We seem to fear the common embarrassed disclaimer as well as the rare swollen head.

Many of us desire praise, but are afraid to seek it. Many of us desire to give praise, but are afraid to express it.

Praise is an under-used tool of awesome power.

TEACHING INFANTS TO SPEAK

To see the power of praise, consider a subject that our society teaches very successfully: teaching infants to speak.

Why do I think we teach this subject well? We get results. Almost all infants succeed in learning.

If you say, "But we don't really teach infants to speak," then I reply that you have just spotlighted a misconception about teaching. Isn't learning the only true indication of good teaching? If they learn from us, we must be teaching them effectively—by definition.

What do we do to help infants learn human language? Equally important, what do we refrain from doing?

When baby says "Mama" for the first time, we do not usually respond with the red-pencil attitude we use so frequently in later education. We don't say, "Incorrect! The word is 'mother.' To make the 'th' sound, put the tip of your tongue against your teeth. Try it again, but this time, concentrate!"

No! If we responded like that, speech would be a rare accomplishment. Fortunately, we respond instead with extravagant praise. We exclaim, " 'Mama!' My baby said, 'Mama'! Oh, I'm so happy I could cry! Just imagine! What a day!"

As a result, baby keeps on speaking. With audience response like this, who would ever leave the stage?

✧ LESSON FROM A MASTER ✧

My great wish was to hear Pablo Casals. One day I met him, but ironically, it was I who had to play. It was in the home of the Von Mendelssohns, a house filled with El Grecos, Rembrandts, and Stradivaris. Francesco von Mendelssohn, a talented cellist, telephoned and asked if he could call for me; they had a guest in the house who would like to hear me play.

"Mr. Casals," I was introduced to a little bald man with a pipe. He said that he was pleased to meet young musicians such as Serkin and me. Rudolph Serkin, who stood stiffly next to me, seemed, like myself, to be fighting his diffidence. Rudi had played before my arrival, and Casals now wanted to hear us together. Beethoven's D-Major Sonata was on the piano. "Why don't you play it?" asked Casals. Both nervous and barely knowing each other, we gave a poor performance that terminated somewhere in the middle.

"Bravo! Bravo! Wonderful!" Casals applauded. Francesco brought the Schumann Cello Concerto, which Casals wanted to hear. I never played worse. Casals asked for Bach. Exasperated, I obliged with a performance matching the others.

"Splendid! *Magnifique!*" said Casals, embracing me. Bewildered, I left the house. I knew how badly I had played, but why did he, the master, have to praise and embrace me? This apparent insincerity pained me more than anything else.

A few years later I met Casals in Paris. We had dinner together and played duets for two cellos, and I played for him until late at night. Spurred by his great warmth and happy, I confessed what I had thought of his praising me in Berlin. He reacted with sudden anger. He rushed to the cello. "Listen!" He played a phrase from the Beethoven sonata. "Didn't you play this fingering? Ah, you did! It was novel to me ... it was good ... and here, didn't you attack that passage with up-bow, like this?" he demonstrated. He went through Schumann and Bach, always emphasizing all he liked that I had done. "And for the rest," he said passionately, "leave it to the ignorant and stupid who judge by counting only the faults. I can be grateful, and so must you be, for even one note, one wonderful phrase." I left with the feeling of having been with a great artist and a friend.

KEEPING THE BALANCE

Our minds seem naturally to focus on difficulties. Undoubtedly, this is a survival tool: it pays to ignore the beautiful scenery and instead focus on the saber-toothed tiger in the bushes. In complex tasks, however, this survival tool can cause an unproductive imbalance in your attention.

Imagine that you just gave a dinner party for ten people. As the first nine left, they said, "The roast beef was delicious!"

As the tenth person left, she said, "The roast beef was delicious! But the string beans were a little burnt."

Later that night, trying to go to sleep, will you be thinking about the roast beef? Probably not. If you're like most of us, you'll be thinking about the string beans. In fact, planning the next dinner party, you may even lose sight of the great pleasure provided by your roast beef, as you focus disproportionately on those pesky string beans and the one unsatisfied person.

To counteract this tendency, we need to hear what we do well about ten times as often as what needs improvement. Otherwise, we tend to forget our true proportion of success to failure.

HOW PRAISE HELPS

Praise has several fundamental roles in the coaching relationship.

First, praise lets people know what they are already doing well. This saves them from wasting time trying to find other ways to succeed at what succeeds already. They can devote their efforts to improving what needs improving and to maintaining what already succeeds.

Second, praise can help people succeed more consistently. If I say, "You followed through on your golf stroke that time," you may learn what it means—and what it feels like—to follow through on your stroke. In the future, you will be more able to recall what you did in your moment of success and to repeat it precisely. Otherwise, you may have to guess—perhaps incorrectly—what it means to "follow through on your stroke."

Third, praise lets people know what comes easily to them. Time and again, recipients of praise respond, "But I wasn't trying hard to accomplish what you mentioned." Like them, you may fail to notice what comes most easily and naturally to you. But the areas where you succeed without effort may represent your greatest strengths. Without praise, you may remain unaware of what you most have to offer.

POSITIVE VS. NEGATIVE

Babies babble. They make many sounds, including sounds that are not used in the language of their culture—such as sounds made while drawing breath in, rather than while forcing breath out. Babies learn from our praise and from our enthusiastic reactions which sounds—of the many they make—have societal value.

One might suppose that we could alternatively communicate to the baby which sounds have value by simply criticizing the sounds that do not have value.

Unfortunately, this critical approach does not work well. The baby can't know that our criticism will stop when he produces a different sound. Since he does not yet know the distinction between the two kinds of sounds, the baby will likely apply our criticism to the making of sound in general. As a result, the baby may stop experimenting with sound altogether.

Thus, while praise is likely to lead to continued experimentation and eventual success, criticism is likely to lead to cessation. It's much more difficult to succeed at what you don't try!

Of course, there are situations in which praise is not the most helpful response available. Several such situations will be described in later chapters. But genuine, discriminating praise is the gold ingot of good coaching: it may not be good for everything, but it can get you further in most circumstances than any other form of currency.

Increase Safety

The coach helps people succeed by helping them learn and grow.

This means that the coach helps people change.

To change is to risk.

The coach can increase the safety of the coaching environment, thus making change less frightening. The process of risking and changing can then proceed at maximum speed.

LEARNING UNDER THE THREAT OF DEATH

Suppose you don't know how to ride a bicycle. Suppose, too, that you are told that you have to learn to ride, but will be shot if you fall off.

How would you approach the learning of this skill, if a mistake would be fatal?

Very cautiously!

It might be possible to learn to ride under these dangerous circumstances. To do so, you would probably spend a long time watching others ride, hoping to learn through observation rather than through experience. You would ask every question you could think of asking. You might even rig up some kind of practice bicycle to allow you to gain parts of the experience without risk of death. You would certainly postpone your first ride until you were sure you had learned everything about bicycling that could be learned without actually riding.

This approach might succeed—but it would be inefficient compared to learning without the artificial threat of being shot. In more ordinary circumstances, you would probably feel free to try riding just as soon as you had asked some basic questions. Once you tried, you'd have new questions to ask and new help to request: "How do I stop? Please be ready to catch me if I can't get off." You would alternate efficiently between observing, asking, and doing. You would have real consequences to confront, of course, if you ran into a wall or fell over—but you would not be concerned with the unnecessary "consequence" of being shot.

My job as a coach is to make it as safe as possible for you, so you can learn without the hindrance of unnecessary consequences.

✧ THE MOMENT THE MASTERPIECE WAS CREATED ✧

Over the gate of the Obaku temple in Kyoto, these words are carved in wood: "The First Principle." This carving is acknowledged as a masterpiece of Japanese calligraphy. Woodcarvers made the carving from a brush drawing by Kosen, who drew the words over 200 years ago.

According to the legend, before beginning his drawing, Kosen asked a student to prepare the supplies. When the calligraphy ink and paper were ready, the student remained—looking over Kosen's shoulder. Kosen wrote the words, "The first principle." The student said, "That is no good."

Kosen wrote the words again. The student responded, "That was no better."

A third time, Kosen drew the words. "That was the worst of all," said the student.

Hours later, eighty-four "first principles" lay on the floor. At this point, the student left the room for a moment. Kosen thought, "Ah! Now is my chance!" Quickly, free from fear of the student's criticism, Kosen wrote once again, "The First Principle." That drawing became the masterpiece.

HOW TO MAKE IT SAFE

To make it safe for you, I can do several things.

First, I can state the principles of coaching. They make it clear that I do not intend to allow several all-too-common but unnecessary consequences of risk-taking: rejoicing in your failures; mocking or usurping your goals; or willfully criticizing or humiliating you.

Second, I can monitor my communications with you to project an atmosphere of trust, tolerance, and interest. I can convey these qualities with words, posture, gesture, and tone of voice.

Third, I can introduce some explicit ground rules that remind us both that a safe atmosphere is important to our work together.

Ground Rules

❋ GROUND RULE #1: YOU ARE IN CHARGE

The first and most important ground rule for emotional safety is to ensure you that you are in charge of what happens in your coaching session. As coach, I am here to help you, but only you actually control what happens.

Being in charge extends to the very smallest detail of your coaching session: where you sit or stand, where I sit or stand, whether you sip tea, whether I take notes, and all other behaviors during your session. Most of these won't matter to you. But if they do, your wishes come first. Of course, if we are in a place that doesn't allow you to bring a beverage inside, for example, we may need to negotiate a satisfactory arrangement for your tea-drinking—whether a new location or a tea break mid-session. But nothing happens without your consent.

Even more importantly, all coaching in your session is subject to your approval. Suppose I suggest, "Would you like to repeat that section of your story so we can see if your improvements have worked?" If, for any reason, you do not want to repeat that section, then you do not repeat it. I can explain why I thought repeating it was potentially useful, but you have absolute veto power.

The importance of this ground rule can hardly be overestimated. You learn best when you feel in charge. Much of your fear associated with being coached actually stems from your prior experiences of being helplessly subjected to the authority of others. If I make it clear that you are in charge, I establish the difference between today's coaching and any earlier painful experiences, and, with one stroke, I rule out the most frightening consequences.

❋ GROUND RULE #2: EVERYTHING YOU SAY IS CONFIDENTIAL

In order to improve, you may need to tell me information about yourself. You may need to think aloud about your goals or personal history as it relates to your presentation. You may need to discuss your own insecurities or negative attitudes. Or the presentation you want to improve may itself be for restricted circulation.

As your coach, I promise you that all such information will remain strictly confidential.

If I did not promise confidentiality, you would have to worry about the consequences of information about you becoming public. With this ground rule in place, however, you need only decide what you want to tell me, not how that information will affect others in your life.

The spread of private information is a real consequence that I can prevent.

Even if I coach you as part of a group, I can insist that all members of the group agree to this ground rule—just as all members of a psychotherapy group may be required to agree to protect the privacy of the others. To make this effective, this ground rule should be announced before anyone has been coached in front of the group.

This ground rule implies that, although participants in a group workshop can make audio or video recordings of their own sessions, they should not record each other's sessions. That way, you will not have to worry about the fate of a tape containing your private information.

In most cases, what you share with me will not be information that you care about keeping private. This is inconsequential. What matters is that you not be distracted by worrying about your privacy.

With confidentiality assured, you can focus on what you need to say, not on who will hear about it later.

❋ GROUND RULE #3: I WON'T REFER TO YOUR PRIOR SESSIONS WITHOUT YOUR PERMISSION

The second ground rule, above, prohibits information from leaving the coaching environment. This third ground rule prohibits information from being referred to later, even within the coaching environment.

Suppose that one day, during a coaching session, you mention that you feel unsure of your abilities. Because of this third ground rule, I won't make reference to those feelings during a later session, unless I first ask your permission. This means that I won't say, out of the blue, "Well, we know you feel unsure of your abilities."

I can refer to those feelings again if I first ask your permission. I may say something like, "Can I refer to something you said two weeks ago?" If you say, "Yes," or "Well, what?" then I can specify: "You had said something about the feelings you had about your abilities." If you still concur, then I can go on. If you demur or hesitate, then I will drop the subject.

Why would I want to establish such a ground rule?

Like the previous ground rule, the rule frees you from unnecessary consequences.

During the session when you said you felt unsure of your abilities, you obviously chose to mention those feelings in order to get just the help you needed. It may have been completely true that you doubted your abilities, or just partly true. You may even have needed to say it aloud, in order to discover that it wasn't really true at all. You did not necessarily choose to be forever known as someone who doubts his abilities. This ground rule prevents that future consequence.

In a group setting, this ground rule is even more important. Suppose this rule were not in place, and group members were free to refer to what you said in your coaching session. Without this ground rule, you might suddenly find yourself identified by other members of the group as someone who doubts his own abilities. What you intended as a statement in the context of being coached has suddenly entered the larger context of the group. You have lost control.

Let us even suppose that your doubts about your abilities are very painful to you. In the safe confines of your coaching session, knowing that your session had a definite time limit and that you had the undivided attention of the group, you chose to mention those painful feelings. Having to face these feelings later, however, in a moment that feels perhaps less safe, is an unnecessary consequence.

With the protection offered by this ground rule, however, you can be assured that only you are in control of which of your feelings, thoughts, and background may be discussed at any particular time. You remain free to share whatever will help you succeed, without concern for any repercussions caused by unrestricted discussion of what you share.

A Structure for Coaching

Just as there are an infinite number of ways to succeed as a storyteller (or baker or consultant), there are an infinite number of ways to succeed at coaching. Each successful coach finds a unique way to incorporate the basic principles of effective coaching.

One possible way to embody the basic principles is to use a four-part structure.

Suppose that you tell a story. To use the four-part structure, I divide my response as coach into as many as four distinct sections. In decreasing order of importance, I listen, I give appreciations, and I give suggestions. Finally, I try to meet any goals of yours that remain.

The first section, listening, always makes sense. Many times, in fact, I will stop there. Other times, I will add appreciations. Less often, I will give suggestions, as well. After completing one or more of these sections, I usually end by attending to any unmet goals of yours.

My most powerful tool is listening. Active, sympathetic listening provides eighty percent of the possible coaching benefit. Happily, such listening provides very little risk: seldom is anyone discouraged after being listened to well.

My next most powerful tool is to give appreciations. About fifteen percent of the potential benefit to you comes from appreciations. Appreciations involve a slightly higher risk than does listening. For example, my appreciations may tempt you to abandon your internal goals in favor of what I seem to like.

The remaining five percent of the time, my suggestions are

invaluable. But suggestions carry the most risk of discouraging you, disempowering you, and consequently inhibiting your creativity and productivity.

Addressing your other goals—the final part of the four-part structure—usually includes elements of all three of the other sections. As a result, it includes the risks and advantages associated with the other three. At the same time, because this part necessarily reminds you that you are in charge of the goals, it carries a smaller risk of disempowering you.

Listening

Like so many of us, I used to take listening for granted, glossing over this step as I rushed into the more active, visible ways of being helpful. Now, I am convinced that listening is the single most important element of any helping relationship.

Listening has great power. It draws thoughts and feelings out of people as nothing else can. When someone listens to you well, you become aware of feelings you may not have realized that you felt. You have ideas you may have never thought before. You become more eloquent, more insightful, more impassioned. You become more yourself.

I once heard someone say, "The way to become smarter tomorrow than you are today is to have someone listen to you as you think aloud." No other tool of the coach can accomplish so much!

The great listeners live blessed lives, because they are surrounded by people under the influence of their listening—people experiencing a fundamental form of connection with others, people whose creativity and humanity have been invited to emerge.

If, as a speaker or performer, you feel even once the effect of a group that is truly listening, you may find yourself seeking that expanded state again and again.

If you feel me listening well, you will be likely to forgive my subsequent bumbles. You will know in your gut that I accept and affirm you, that I seek to learn more of who you are and what you have to offer. You will know that you have found in me not a judge or an opponent but a helper.

The great power of listening is nearly ignored in our society. If someone could sell a machine or prescribe a pill that could be equally effective in human growth, it would be advertised on every television show. Fortunately, the power of listening can be available free to everyone.

HOW TO LISTEN

Good listening is not only auditory. It requires at least three senses, as well as compassion and intellect.

If you tell a story or make a speech, I use my ears, of course. I listen to your words. I also listen to your tone of voice, with its rich emotional potential. I even listen to your silences. Different silences have different qualities—from expectant to teasing, from restful to reactive—which I can learn to hear.

I also listen with my eyes. I watch your face, your gestures, your position in the room, and your posture. I watch your eyes, noticing when your gaze meets mine, when it focuses on an imagined object, or when it shifts to the side as you recall a memory or try to formulate a thought.

I listen with my own muscles and posture. I relax. I face you. Unconsciously, I match some of your muscular tensions with my own, thus experiencing some of your internal, physical state. I may even match my breathing to yours, to try to feel your inner rhythms, the tidal motion of your lungs. If it helps me, I take notes, giving myself a chance to register my experience of you both in language and in the movement of my writing hand.

With my compassion, I try to imagine what emotional state in you might give rise to what I see, hear, and feel. I try to enter your attitude, to inhabit your intention. I accept whatever I discover.

With my intellect, I try to follow your train of thought, noting the sidetracks, the loading stations, and the main line. I attempt to see things from your point of view. I endeavor to distinguish the kernel of your intention, even as I accept your nervous jokes, your incidental digressions, your apologies, your defenses-in-advance. I notice the connections among the topics and images you present, and the progressions from one to another. I listen to understand.

I devote all my attention to you. For this period of time, you are the most important thing to me in the world.

HOW TO RESPOND WHILE LISTENING

While listening to you as your coach, I receive your communication on many levels. At the same time, I also communicate my response to you.

I encourage you to continue, by facing you. I show my attention and respect by alternately meeting your gaze and averting my eyes, as appropriate. (The meaning of eye contact depends on many factors, including culture, setting, and our relationship.)

I respond to your pauses, gestures, and words with appropriate grunts, exclamations, sighs, and laughs, as well as with nods, shrugs, and tilts of my head.

As a listener, I also signal my response through facial expressions. When I myself perform, my favorite listener to have in my audience is Brother Blue, a Boston-based professional storyteller. When Brother Blue listens, his face dances to the story's silent music, mirroring the constantly mutating emotions of the narrative. His face draws my best out of me as a storyteller.

As a good listener, I respond to your requests. Your requests may be explicit, such as "Try to make the sound that Coyote made when he was trapped under the boulder," or "Give me a minute here to catch my breath!" Requests may also be elliptical, as when you say "Just ..." in a tone of voice that suggests "Just a minute, please." And requests may be only implied, conveyed by devices such as a wrinkling of the forehead, a raising of a finger, or a verbal place-holder like "Uh ..." which communicates a request not to be interrupted.

HOW NOT TO RESPOND

As a helpful listener, I do not interrupt you.

I do not give advice.

I do not do something else while listening to you. I do not convey distraction through nervous mannerisms.

I do not finish your sentences for you. In spite of all my attempts to understand you, I do not assume I know what you mean.

I do not convey disapproval, impatience, or condescension. If I am confused, I show a desire for clarification, not dislike for your obtuseness. I do not act vindicated when you misspeak or correct yourself.

I do not sit impassively, withholding participation.

Instead, I project affection, approval, interest, and enthusiasm. I am your servant, your booster, your partner in communication. I am eager for your imminent success, fascinated by your struggles, forgiving of your mistakes, always expecting the best. I am your delighted listener.

WHAT INTRUDES ON MY ABILITY TO LISTEN

When I agree to coach you, I agree that, for the period of your coaching session, your needs take precedence over mine. Coaching you may, in fact, meet my needs even as it meets yours, but if a conflict arises between meeting my needs and meeting yours, I agree to postpone my needs (see "The Coaching Agreement," page 225).

When I fail to listen well, this means either that I do not understand my role, or that a need of my own has taken precedence over my commitment to you.

Of course, I do not deserve reproach for my failures, any more than you do. Yet, if I can notice what intrudes, I may be more able to postpone my needs until it is my turn to meet them—either alone or with help from a willing helper. I may be able to recognize my needs and temporarily give them their appropriate backseat—before they actually intrude.

If I am able to recognize my needs but not postpone them, I

can at least tell you. I can even renegotiate our "contract," saying, "Something just came up for me. I think I need to stop for a while. Can we take a break now?"

In general, my intrusive needs are of two kinds.

First, the role of coach itself may be frightening, unnerving, or burdensome to me. In my desire not to fail, I may rush to action instead of listening patiently and imaginatively. In my uncertainty about my own abilities, I may seize the first response that comes into my head and pursue it desperately, fearing that no other thought will ever present itself. In my weariness, I may unconsciously disengage, protecting myself against what feels like unfair demands. Even the role of listener itself may feel uncomfortable—if, for example, I was previously deprived of such listening or was forced to listen to others beyond my capacity.

Second, you may have touched on a subject that reminds me of my own emotional sore spots, unrelated to my role as coach. This reminder may prompt me to want to tell you about my hurt—either directly, by talking about it, or indirectly, by assuming an attitude of a victim or a victimizer.

Thus, I may find myself launching into a story about my own similar or dissimilar experiences—a story that is intended more to relieve me than to assist you. Or my tone might shift to an edgy disapproval of some aspect of your story or presentation, as though you were just one more in the series of nasty people who have infringed on my psychic space.

Alternatively, the subject you have raised may prompt me to try to escape from my discomfort into the role of the victimizer. For example, if you express a cheerful, innocent optimism that reminds me of my similar attitude as a child, I may unconsciously seek to avoid a repetition of how my optimism was invalidated, by taking the role of invalidator toward you. Suddenly, I may find myself seized with the urge to warn you of the painful disappointments that await you unless you adopt a more "realistic" attitude—just as others, long ago, may have discouraged me from hoping.

The needs that distract me may not be as dramatic as those

in the previous examples. All through my life, for example, I have developed useful mental and emotional shortcuts that meet my need to ignore repetitive detail. I have learned to categorize things and people in order not to deal with them individually every time I see a billboard or pass a stranger in the street. To coach you, however, I need to put aside some of my preconceptions, my habitual responses, my ordinary need to view the world in categories. I need to open myself to your individuality.

DEALING WITH MY NEEDS AS COACH

I have two kinds of tools for dealing with my various intrusive needs.

First, I can—before or after your coaching session—arrange for the appropriate meeting of my needs. I can eat a snack, take a nap, or call my children. I can tell my own story, get others to appreciate me, or take a long walk that connects me with nature. I can process my fear, grieve my losses, or open myself to my frightening vulnerability. Once my real needs are met, they will not be there to intrude. In this way, it is part of my role as helper to make sure that I meet my own needs.

Second, I can remind myself of my commitment to you, and rededicate myself to the helper role. Very few actual needs are so strong that they can't be held off for an hour or a day to be spent in the role of helper—provided that I acknowledge their existence, have some hope of meeting them later, and decide to act, for the meanwhile, on my commitment to you as your coach.

I can decide, once again, to listen.

✧ RISING ABOVE IT ✧

Once there was a Zen master who lived near a small village in Japan.

Whenever the local villagers found themselves bogged down by worries or obsessed with their sorrows, they went to the monastery and sought the Zen master. He would listen to them, sometimes for many hours.

As they would turn to leave, relieved of their emotional burden, he would say, "I think you have risen above it."

One day, three of the villagers were traveling in a neighboring town. Passing a house, they heard the sounds of mourning. One voice, in particular, was wailing more woefully than all the others.

Entering the house to investigate, they saw that the loud weeping voice belonged to the Zen master!

The villagers confronted him. "You tell us to rise above our passion, yet here you are, crying louder than any of us."

The Zen master stopped his weeping for a moment and smiled. "Yes. This is how I rise above it."

Appreciations

Listening is always appropriate. As your coach, many times I will do nothing but listen.

When it makes sense to go beyond listening, however, my next step is appreciations.

By "appreciations," I mean praise: telling you what went well in your story (or what seems effective in your business plan or oil painting).

In most cases, it is important for me to give praise first. Usually, the first question on your mind is, "Did I succeed at all?" Until you receive an answer, you may be preoccupied with this basic question and have trouble absorbing other information.

Further, appreciations help you determine which of your goals were achieved and valued. If I mention your main goals positively, you are free to discuss other issues. If I do not, you can ask immediately whether they were achieved—and, if necessary, you can devote your primary attention to them.

Why Give Appreciations All Together?

Appreciations are grouped together (rather than interspersed among suggestions) for two reasons.

The lesser reason is to assist those giving appreciations, whether me as an individual coach or a group of your peers.

We have a destructive cultural habit of saying, "I liked your story, but ...." Although the words may seem to say "I liked your story," the tone of voice communicates, "I'm about to criticize you, but I'm being considerate and giving you a moment to brace yourself."

When I separate appreciations from other responses, I am more likely to notice whether my tone implies a "but ..." and thus is not an appreciation at all.

The second, greater reason for grouping appreciations together is to assist you.

Your job as a receiver of appreciations is to open yourself to them. They are not to be adjusted, corrected, or negotiated. Appreciations are to be accepted as absolute truth.

If I say to you, "Your story moved me to tears," you must accept my response. It does not matter that you did things better yesterday, or that you forgot the most important part of the story, or that you usually get a better response from the CEO. If I was moved to tears, your only helpful response is to accept that I was moved to tears. You have an obligation to absorb my honest response to your story or other presentation.

Absorbing praise is not easy. We have emotional armor that protects us from hurts but also intercepts praise. To let in praise, we must temporarily open a gap in our emotional protections.

It is much easier to hold open such a gap if we know that, until further notice, the only thing aimed at us will be praise.

✧ ELLIOT COLEMAN'S GIFT ✧

When I was a student at Johns Hopkins University, I wanted to join a poetry writing course taught by professor Elliot Coleman. To be accepted into the course, first I had to show Coleman a sample of my poetry. Fearing criticism, I procrastinated.

When at last I braved an appointment with him and let him read my poems, I was astonished at his response: he told me what he liked about them. I left his office buoyed and inspired. That very week I wrote a poem that broke new ground for me.

When my poems were discussed in class, I often felt that Coleman understood my purposes better than I did. I always left class inspired and able to improve what I had written.

One week, I lingered in Professor Coleman's classroom after the class session had ended. All had left the room except two other students, on whom I was eavesdropping.

One of the students was attacking a poem that the other had written. At bay, the author of the poem defended himself: "Well, Elliot Coleman likes this poem!"

The other, arching for the kill, hissed, "So? Elliot Coleman likes everything!"

In that moment, I understood two things. Of course, I understood what the attacker meant: if I like everything equally, my judgment is meaningless.

But I also understood what the attacker did not. Elliot Coleman did not praise indiscriminately. On the contrary, his great gift was his ability to find what there was to like in every poem he read.

HOW TO GIVE APPRECIATIONS

Since our society is so squeamish about giving praise, most of us have not developed this art to fullness. It takes practice to become expert at this fundamental coaching skill.

First of all, good praise is always honest. The power of praise cannot be realized through lies. Don't feel you have to invent praise. In time, you will develop your ability to find and report honestly that which is praiseworthy.

Second, good praise responds to the needs of the person being praised.

When I was a preschool teacher, children would hold their

fresh paintings up for me to see. I soon learned that different children wanted different responses.

If I tried a blanket response of "That's nice," some children would go away satisfied; others would leave disappointed. Others tried to teach me how to respond. They would wait expectantly while I tried other responses, leaving only after I hit upon what they wanted.

Still other children prompted me to give the praise they needed, saying, perhaps, "I made a big monster!" If I took the cue and said something like, "That is a huge, brown monster! It covers half the page," they would leave satisfied and return to their work. If that response was still off the mark, they would help me further: "It's scary!" Then I knew to say, "That is a very scary monster. I'm getting scared just looking at it!"

From these children, I learned that appreciations come in several forms. I also learned some categories of praise and how to give it in a variety of helpful ways.

GLOBAL PRAISE AND SPECIFIC PRAISE

Some helpful praise is global or general. I might say to the preschool artist, "That is a beautiful picture!" or "You are a good artist!" To the storyteller, I might say, "What a wonderful performance!" or "I love that story!"

Some praise is specific, spelling out, "Look at all the black in that picture!" or "I like how you filled in the whole sky with clouds!" For the storyteller, I might specify, "You achieved a balance between the contrariness of the Maine farmer and your love for him as your grandfather," or "I loved the phrase, 'It was the way someone thanks you when they hate you.' "

Specific praise can run the gamut from individual details to praise for imagery, character, or structure. Some writing groups have reported good results from a very restricted form of specific appreciation. In this form, the coach mentions only the exact words of another's story that made an impact on the coach.

PRAISING THE OBJECT, THE PERFORMER, OR THE EFFECT

Whether global or specific, some praise focuses primarily on the work of art or the event itself. Examples of this kind of praise are, "What a great picture!" or "What a tender, sweet story!" Of course, such praise can also be specific: "Your picture has so much green in it!" or "The scene where you fall into the water is a classic!"

Some praise, however, focuses on the artist or presenter. "You know how to boss that brush around!" or "You have a gift for showing us the humor in a tragic situation." Again, this can be specific: "You know how to mix two colors to make a new one!"

Still other praise focuses on the effect on the audience. "That picture makes me feel happy all over!" or "I'm still laughing inside as I think about your uncle!" As always, such appreciations can be specific ("Something about that yellow circle gives me a tickled feeling.") or general ("I could listen to you for hours!").

Only by having all these forms of praise in my repertory can I hope to notice and express that which you most need me to mention.

EXAMPLES OF THE KINDS OF APPRECIATION

... ABOUT THE EFFECT ON THE OBSERVER

GLOBAL APPRECIATIONS:

- That tickled me!
- That moved me!
- That made me think ...
- I enjoyed listening to you.
- What a great ... (e.g., experience, way to spend an hour).

SPECIFIC APPRECIATIONS:

- I laughed so hard when ...
- I was there with you when ...
- The phrase ... gave me a new way to think about ...

... ABOUT THE STORY

GLOBAL APPRECIATIONS:

- What a great ... (e.g., story, example of oral literature, expression of the immigrant experience)!
- What a beautiful ...!
- What a clever ...!
- What a moving ...!

SPECIFIC APPRECIATIONS:

- What an unforgettable ... (e.g., character, scene, turn of plot)!
- I loved the way you said, "...."
- The story made a clear progression from ... to ...

... ABOUT THE STORYTELLER

GLOBAL APPRECIATIONS:

- You are an effective ... (e.g., storyteller, performer, communicator).
- Keep up the good work!
- You were clearly speaking from your heart!

SPECIFIC APPRECIATIONS:

- You know how to ...
- It's a difficult task to .... And you did it!
- You have solved the problem of ...
- You ... (e.g., enunciate, take pauses, portray characters) well.

✧ A WORD AND A SENTENCE ✧

In the early 1930s, Mischa Borodkin was already an established symphony violinist when he decided to study conducting under the foremost teacher of conducting in the world, Felix Weingartner.

Screwing up his courage, he journeyed to Switzerland during the symphonic off-season and presented himself to Maestro Weingartner.

"Maestro, I'm not sure I belong here. Everyone else seems to have studied conducting already. I have not."

Weingartner looked at this student, who, at age thirty,

had already played in the New York Philharmonic for twelve years. "Very well, you will conduct first. Prepare a piece for tomorrow, and we'll see if you belong here."

Late into the night, Mischa prepared his first work to conduct.

The next morning, as the last note of Beethoven's Coriolanus Overture died out, Mischa looked anxiously at the conductor. Weingartner spoke the single most important word a teacher can say: "Stay!"

At the end of the summer course, Weingartner bid goodbye to Mischa with a memorable sentence of encouragement: "Write me of your success in America!"

Weingartner did not say, "You are a great conductor," nor even, "You have made great progress." He did not evaluate Mischa at all. His gift of a single sentence was much greater, because this appreciation told Mischa that Weingartner believed in him.

Of all his stories from his nearly fifty-year musical career, Mischa told this one with the greatest sense of pride.

GIVING THANKS

While I am appreciating the presenter, the presentation, and the effect on you, I might also express my gratitude.

Giving thanks is not quite the same as other forms of appreciation. It acknowledges your efforts or their good effects:

- I am grateful for what you did (or thought, offered, or noticed).
- I am grateful for your effect on me.
- I am grateful for your good intentions.
- I am grateful for the opportunity to be your coach.

My gratitude can be global or specific:

- Thanks for telling that story!
- Thanks for portraying such a modest dimension to a hero!

Some people have received enough thanks, but not enough

appreciation of their good qualities. Still others have been told how effective they are, but they hunger to have their efforts acknowledged.

Gratitude is almost always appropriate. Even the least successful efforts can be positively acknowledged through thanks.

Giving thanks cannot substitute for the other forms of appreciation, but—for a particular person at a particular moment—it can be the most important form.

TONING UP OUR PRAISE

The content of appreciations is important. Even more important, however, is the tone of voice with which praise is given.

Any appreciation can be said in a tone of voice that conveys any emotion. As every actor knows, "I like your story" can be said with a vocal intonation that carries a range of meanings from "I idolize you" to "I can't stand having you around."

As a result, the most effective coach will use nonverbal cues to give emotional force to appreciations. Some of the many appropriate flavors of praise are joy, impish delight, awe, admiration, gleeful surprise, and pride. The most effective coach can express any of these nonverbally, through facial expression, posture, and gesture, as well as through tone of voice.

WHAT IF THERE IS NOTHING TO PRAISE?

People sometimes ask, "But what if a performance is just awful? What if there is nothing good about it? How can I give honest appreciation then?"

My answer has three parts. First, the habit of paying attention to difficulties (mentioned in "Keeping the Balance," page 38) can make it hard for me as your coach to think about what is praiseworthy when I am faced with a looming, annoying deficiency. The problem in this case, however, is not that there is nothing to praise, but that I cannot take my attention off the defect long enough to notice what worked well.

Practice can make it easier for me to pay attention to the good in your performance. It may even help for me to tell the story (privately, not in my role as coach) of anyone in my past who might have seen only my shortcomings. Such inflexibility in directing my attention usually stems from some unhealed emotional hurt of my own. (See "Heal the Hurt," page 161.)

Second, once I have unlocked my attention from the deficiencies, I can try to look systematically at your story, at you as the performer, and at your effect on the audience. I can ask myself for each of these categories whether there is something general or specific to appreciate. In most cases, I will find abundant merit, however covered with dross.

Third, in the very rare case where you are actually failing on all fronts, I can find something laudable in your goals.

I remember once beginning a session of appreciations by asking, "What do you love about that story?"

The answer came, "It shows how we can respond to threatening situations without violence."

I had certainly not received the intended message from the story as performed. But I could easily appreciate the goal, saying, "That's a wonderful thing to show! That intention is very close to my heart! Thank you for choosing such an important story!" Later, I helped the storyteller better achieve her goal. But for now, I could enthusiastically appreciate her intentions.

When Appreciations Are Enough

In many cases, I follow the giving of appreciations with the next two parts of the four-part structure. Often, though, it makes sense for me to stop after giving appreciations.

If I am leading a group—such as a group of young children—where giving appreciations is itself a big challenge, it might not make sense to go on to suggestions on the same day or even in the same year.

Giving appreciations can be an intellectual challenge for those very young or very inexperienced at speaking praise. It can also be an emotional challenge for those in situations which do not feel safe. I think immediately of certain groups of adolescents for whom trying to humiliate each other is part of their accepted "group culture." I think also of adult prison inmates for whom telling a story to their peers is by itself unthinkably bold.

In situations such as these, it may be too much—at first—to ask group members even to appreciate each other. I can still begin to teach the skills of appreciation, however. I can offer appreciations myself to those who try a story and agree to hear my praise.

I can also let a group coach me. This way, any inappropriate or hostile comments will not be aimed at someone who needs my protection. Now, I am in a position to coach the group—on their appreciations! I can commend them when they appreciate well, praise the core of appreciation in a mixed message, and respond honestly to any attempts to make me feel bad. (For more specific techniques for letting students coach you and for coaching them on their appreciations, see pages 212-213.)

Even in groups of advanced storytellers and skilled coaches, however, there are times to stop after the giving of appreciations.

Many of us, for example, have been trained to please others—to the point that the "inner voice" of our own intention is easily drowned out. In this case, a coach's suggestions—no matter how gently phrased—may speak too loudly in our ears.

Brand new creations may also require special treatment. When I am being coached myself, I have found that when I first tell a new story, sing a new song, or think aloud about the idea for a new book, the only helpful responses are appreciations. I think of such stories, songs or ideas as "babies." All I really want to know is, "will this baby live?" I do not yet want extended advice about diaper services, or moving to an excellent school district, or how to deal with the high school years. Pointing to future problems at this point will only overwhelm me. Therefore, I have learned to take charge of my time being coached by accepting only praise—of anything in the "baby" that touched or pleased someone or seemed alive.

✧ THE TEACHER'S RESTRAINT ✧

Mr. Rambus had given us an extra-credit problem in high school geometry. It involved constructing a particular line within a trapezoid. Most of us were stumped. He continued to smile his enigmatic smile as we suffered.

Five of us seemed to have some idea how to proceed. I later learned that the other four were solving the problem the way Mr. Rambus had solved it—but that I was approaching it in a completely different way.

I worked for fifteen minutes, then got stuck. I wrote part of a formula on a piece of paper, which I showed to Mr. Rambus, saying, "I can construct all of it except this one piece. Is there any way to construct this expression?"

He smiled as he always did, then said, "I think you're on to something!"

Those six words were as remarkable for what they omitted as for what they included. After all, he might have told me that I was approaching the problem all wrong. Or he might have reminded me, "Don't you remember? We constructed that expression a month ago." More benignly, he might have reassured me, "Yes, there is a way." Any of those responses could have led me to a correct answer. But none of them would have left me with the feeling of encouragement and accomplishment that I soon received.

Buoyed by his expression of belief in me, I took another look at the expression I had written down. Of course! This expression was equivalent to another problem we had already solved. I constructed it easily, then finished the extra-credit problem.

Mr. Rambus had guided me toward something greater than a right answer: toward the exhilaration of finding an answer that was all my own.

Suggestions

Obviously, devoting one part of the four-part structure to appreciations is a direct application of the basic principle, "give praise." Given, too, that people respond to appreciations in a unique way, it makes sense to restrict that part to appreciations.

As important as listening and appreciations are, however, they are not the only ways for a coach to be helpful. Sometimes it makes sense for me to go on to give suggestions, which are explicit thoughts about making a story (or any kind of presentation or project) better.

WHY GIVE SUGGESTIONS ALL TOGETHER?

Appreciations, as discussed above, are best received as truth. Suggestions, on the other hand, are to be received like shopping coupons: use what you can, but don't hesitate to throw the rest away.

When it is your turn to receive suggestions, think of yourself as a queen being offered gifts by your humble but devoted subjects.

When your eager subjects place their gifts at your feet, your royal manners require you to smile and say thank you to each gift. If you have questions about the gifts from your subjects, of course, you ask them: "Are these goblets ornamental or to drink from?"

As queen, you have no further obligations. You don't have to explain why a gift isn't what you want. You certainly don't have to defend your reputation against implied aspersions: "What? How dare you offer me plastic goblets! What kind of a palace do you think I run here?" You may choose to use a gift, of course, but you can also put it in the royal storeroom, throw it in the fire, or give it to the needy in the next kingdom.

My suggestions about your story are offerings to you. You are the only judge of their usefulness.

By devoting a time period to suggestions, I help you separate suggestions both from listening and from appreciations, each of which requires a different attitude on your part. You reach out to me when I listen; you are open to me when I appreciate you; but you sit securely on your throne of judgment when I offer you suggestions.

THE KINDS OF SUGGESTIONS

There are three basic kinds of helpful suggestions.

The first kind of helpful suggestion is an idea that you might implement. Such a suggestion can begin with the words, "I wonder if your story might be even better if ...."

Of course, you have no obligation to try such a suggestion, but it is stated as a clear alteration to your story (or your business plan or quilt design) that you *could* make—if you judge that it would actually be an improvement.

The second kind of "suggestion" consists of a statement of my own reaction. This might begin, "I felt confused when ...," or "I found myself rooting for the hero's enemy at this point ...." As always, you have no obligation to change your story based on my reaction. Nonetheless, it may prove helpful to you to know that one listener reacted in a particular way.

The third kind of helpful "suggestion" is a question. The question brings answers from you, not from me. No other form of suggestion is so inherently respectful of your creativity.

Each form of suggestion has uses and risks. To maximize their effectiveness, I need to know not only how to create each form, but also how to translate the kernel of a suggestion from one form to another.

❋ KINDS OF SUGGESTIONS #1: MAKING A POSITIVE SUGGESTION

A positive suggestion, as defined here, is an alternative that you *might* choose, not a correction that you *should* choose. It is phrased in a way that expands your concept of what is possible, but makes clear that you retain the power to choose.

A positive suggestion might be phrased in one of these ways:

- I wonder if your presentation might be even better if you ....
- What if you ...?
- When you said, "...," I thought you were going to add, "...."

- Would you like to hear my fantasy of the ending? I have the image in my mind that … might happen.
- You solved the problem of … by …. Another way to solve the same problem might be to ….

If I dislike the bird sounds in your story, I have the opportunity to make a suggestion about improving it. I might say:

- I wonder if the story might be even better if you described the bird sounds instead of imitating them.
- After your description of the bird sounds, I expected something very delicate. Is there a way to give your whistling sound a more delicate quality?
- The way you described the bird sounds as "delicate trillings" made me imagine something that was even more beautiful than your whistling. What if you omitted the whistling and allowed us to imagine the sound of the birds?

A positive suggestion is not advice. A positive suggestion does not say:

- You should ….
- I would ….
- A better way to do this is to ….
- Stories are supposed to ….
- Bird sounds don't belong in a story.

A positive suggestion is not a command. It does *not* sound like one of these:

- Never …!
- Find a better setting for the opening!
- Get rid of those bird sounds!

A positive suggestion is not a comparison. It does not invoke an authority or master storyteller for you to imitate—or with whom to avoid similarities. (Remember, though, that turning to masters for inspiration is very different from being compared to them.) A positive suggestion does not take one of these forms :

- You know who does this kind of story the best? Hemingway. Try to be more like him.

- Don't try that unless you're a Hemingway.
- Try not to be so much like Hemingway.
- The man who could *really* do bird sounds was Hemingway.

✧ THE FAMOUS STORY I WILL NEVER READ ✧

I was once a student in a creative writing graduate program. In the first semester, I showed the writer in residence—a noted critic—a short story I had written.

His comment was, "This is a story about dementia praecox. I'm writing down for you the name of a famous story that treats this subject successfully. I suggest you read it."

I skimmed the story he recommended, but was distracted by a feeling like jealousy. Discouraged and deprived of help, I put my own short story on the bottom of a pile.

To this day, I have never wanted to read the story that he recommended.

In the second semester, our new writer in residence was novelist George Garrett. He seemed so friendly that I showed him my now stagnant story.

He responded by saying, "When the heroine of a story goes through a psychological difficulty, we'll follow her trials if we care about her. I wonder—could you add an incident at the beginning that would make us like her?"

By the time I went to sleep that night, I had written a draft of a new opening to my story. Given a problem to solve, my energies had been mobilized. The story was improved. I also learned a principle about helping my readers like my characters, which I have since been able to apply to many stories.

Furthermore, a positive suggestion is specific enough to help you imagine an alternative to your existing presentation. It gives a possible solution, not just a problem. It does *not* say:

- Good stories have three-dimensional characters.

- I wonder if you could improve the ending.
- The bird sounds don't work.

The positive suggestion is defined as much by your tone of voice as by the words you say. Your tone does not say, "I have the answer," or "You'd better ...." Your tone asks, "Would this idea help any?"

If, as your coach, I cannot put my thoughts about improving your presentation into a positive suggestion, then I should put them into a statement of my personal reaction, or into questions—as discussed in the next sections.

If I can't put them into one of these three forms, it is almost always better for me to say nothing than to give advice, make a command, or deliver a non-specific suggestion. These latter responses of mine are quite likely to disempower or discourage you.

Discouraging you completely is the worst thing I can do. If you go into the world telling a story with a flaw in it, you may very well find someone else who can help you change it, or you might even fix it yourself. Only if you give up completely is there no hope of your success.

✵ Kinds of Suggestions #2: Stating My Own Reaction

Once I told a Jewish mystical story on the radio. One character in the story, whom I identified only as "a bishop," is violently anti-Semitic. After the broadcast, a listener called up to say, "I loved your story. I just wanted you to know that I went to a Catholic school, and the Jesuit teachers always told us that the Jews are the chosen people. We were taught to look up to Jews."

After hearing this listener's reaction, I realized that he had felt, in some way, that I was painting all Catholics with the brush of my character's prejudice. This was not my intention in telling the story. As a result, I changed the "bishop" into a less-specific "high priest of that land."

The listener had not made a "suggestion" in the usual sense of the word. Nevertheless, hearing his reaction made me understand how I wanted to change my story. Without making me defensive or threatening my artistic control of my story, he gave me information that helped me make my story more effective.

Further, he taught me about a new kind of helpful suggestion, in which I, as coach, simply state my individual reaction to what I heard. In other words, I state my experience as your listener.

Of course, you are never obligated to change your story or proposal based on my reactions. Yet the reactions of your listeners are the primary measure of your success. As a result, knowing more about such reactions may cause you to rethink your communicative strategy.

Here are some sample individual reactions I can give that might be helpful:

- I felt confused when you said, "...."
- I found myself worrying about ....
- At the point in the story when ..., I felt ....
- I found myself distracted by ....
- When you said, "...," I thought of ....
- When you said, "...," I was taken out of your story while I changed my mental image of ..., which I had earlier imagined as ....

Note that all these reactions are phrased as statements about me, not about you or about your presentation.

As your coach, I must be on guard against making evaluative statements in the guise of statements about my reaction. The following statements are thinly disguised criticisms:

- I feel that your story is more of a lecture than a real story.
- When you said, "...," I thought, "This is boring."
- My reaction was confusion: why would you bother me with this drivel?

These statements are actually evaluations of you or your presentation. Like all such statements, they tend to put you in the role of the receiver of evaluation, rather than in the more productive role of creative problem-solver.

This form of suggestion is especially helpful when, like my Catholic radio listener, I find myself feeling stereotyped by a story or other presentation. You may—justly—feel chastised if I say, "That story was oppressive of men," or even, "Your story promulgates the mistaken notion that men are just beasts whose instincts must be kept under control." But you may be more able to respond with understanding if I say, "As a man, I kept feeling like saying, 'But I believe that my deepest instincts are good, not beast-like!' "

Occasionally, I can even succeed in invoking the reactions of other people. I can say, "As I listened to your story, I kept thinking of my friend Rita, and imagining her reaction. I have heard her say, 'As an African-American, I'm so tired of hearing the color black associated with evil.' "

In this way, I can sometimes alert you to aspects of your presentation that may be offensive to others, without making sweeping statements that may leave you feeling blamed or reprimanded.

Statements about my reaction also keep you focused on communicating to me. When you hear me say, "I thought you said 'on tide,' rather than 'untied,' " you have new information about my reaction as a listener. Your most likely course of action, once you have understood my confusion, is to clarify what you meant, now and in the future. When you tell the same story later, you will probably make some change to prevent that misunderstanding. You might pronounce "untied" more carefully, or rephrase to "was untying," or make some other equally effective change—you might even make a change each time you tell the story.

When, on the other hand, I make a statement about you or your story—such as, "Your pronunciation of those words was unclear," or "Your story had a confusing phrase in it"—you are less likely to make a flexible, matter-of-fact improvement in your story. You may find yourself thinking reactively about *being* "unclear" rather than proactively about *saying* "untied." In short, when I make a statement about you or your story, I direct your focus to protecting yourself or your creation. The resulting defensiveness can interfere with your communication.

A statement of my reaction allows me to alert you to any unintended effects of your story—without making you defensive—even if I am unable to convert my reactions into positive suggestions or questions.

❋ KINDS OF SUGGESTIONS #3: ASKING QUESTIONS

It may seem odd to classify questions as a form of "suggestion." Yet they rank as my most powerful kind of tool for drawing on your creativity while directing you toward specific improvements.

Questions point you toward answers within you, the storyteller—not within me, the coach.

Questions can be categorized by their form as well as by their content. The form of a question can be open-ended or closed-ended. The content can point toward the coaching session itself, toward your intentions, or toward the structure and substance of your story or project. Each type of question has advantages and drawbacks.

Most often, I formulate a series of questions in response to a hypothesis I am forming about your story. As you answer these questions, I confirm or change my hypothesis while simultaneously relating it to your goals.

OPEN-ENDED AND CLOSED-ENDED QUESTIONS

Closed-ended questions direct you to a specific answer. They ask for a particular piece of information, such as:

- How old was that character?
- What did you want to accomplish with that prop?
- Did you say 'on tide' or 'untied'?
- Would you like to continue with this exercise?

Closed-ended questions have certain characteristics. They direct your attention to a precise fact. They allow me to verify my understanding of what you have said or intended. They clarify.

Closed-ended questions can be reassuring. You don't need to make complicated judgments before answering them. They make your side of the conversation simple.

Closed-ended questions also discourage narrative. If you are in the middle of a long explanation or story and I ask a closed-ended question, it makes you stop to answer. If I ask three or four such questions in a row, it may stop the whole explanation.

To get facts, I ask closed-ended questions. To get stories, on the other hand, I ask questions that are open-ended. If closed-ended questions are like spotlights, illuminating just an actor's face or hands, open-ended questions are like floodlights, shining on the whole stage.

Open-ended questions direct you to a wide range of possible answers. They ask for non-specific information, such as:

- What can you tell me about that character?
- Tell me about that prop. What meanings does it have for you?
- Are there other times when you felt that way as a child?
- What else would you like from us?

Open-ended questions invite narrative. They encourage you to explore.

If I want to know something specific, an open-ended question is a very inefficient tool. It prolongs the conversation. If I am not ready for a long answer, asking you an open-ended question and not staying around for the extended response may leave you with the feeling that I am not really interested in you.

Open-ended questions require you to make multiple decisions before answering. You have to decide how much of the answer to include. This forces you to make judgments about my goals: "Why do you want to know?" If you are feeling safe and accepted, open-ended questions can make you feel that I am deeply interested in you. If you are not feeling safe, they can feel like dangerous probes into uncertain territory.

In the educational system of my childhood, open-ended questions were rare. Few people gained experience in asking or answering them. Even "essay questions" were often closed-ended, since they requested specific—if extensive—information. I learned to find the hidden close-ended question within the apparently open-ended one.

As a result, I grew up less conversant with open-ended questions. I have had to make a conscious effort to ask them, and to notice when you interpret my questions as more close-ended than I intend. In fact, I may need to follow an open-ended question with further prompts, just to clarify that my question was not a close-ended one in disguise:

- Tell me more.
- Say whatever thought comes into your mind.
- Just tell me anything you remember on that topic.
- I'm just interested in knowing what you think about that.

For an open-ended question to have its desired effect, both of us must recognize it for what it is.

WHAT DOES THE QUESTION ASK ABOUT?

Questions—whether open- or closed-ended—can ask about the coaching session itself, as when I ask you, "Would you like to hear what we like about your story?" These questions are described more fully in "Asking Permission" (page 84).

Questions can also ask about your intentions, as when I ask, "What do you love about your story?" These questions are central to the chapter, "Needing More Experience of the Story (page 111).

Still other questions ask about the content or structure of your story: "In your opinion, was Jack surprised when he saw the beanstalk grow?" or "What do you see as the climax of your story?" These are discussed in "Questions: The Tool of Choice" (page 130).

USING QUESTIONS TO EXPLORE A HYPOTHESIS

If I suspect that your version of "Jack and the Beanstalk" needs a more terrifying portrayal of the giant, I can use questions to establish whether such a change would, in fact, further your goals.

I can start by asking about your main goals:

QUESTION 1. *"Why do you love this story?" or "What makes you want to tell this story?"*

If you answer, "I love how plucky Jack is," I may think to myself, "Aha, that's what I suspected! Now let's get him a worthy enemy by making the giant more scary."

Out loud, I can ask:

QUESTION 2. *"What does Jack do that is so plucky?" or "Where does Jack's pluckiness show up in the story?"*

If you answer, "Well, he goes back up the beanstalk a second and a third time," I may think, "Precisely! And it wouldn't be plucky if the giant were kindly and offered him cookies!"

Out loud, I can continue asking:

QUESTION 3. *"Why is it plucky for him to go up again?"*

You might answer, "He knows he might get killed!"

Then I can ask so you verify what I've learned from you, "So you love Jack's pluck in going back up the beanstalk, even though he knows he might get killed?"

If you agree, then I can make a straightforward suggestion based on my confirmed hypothesis: "I wonder if it would make Jack's pluckiness even clearer if the giant were clearly dangerous. Could you make the giant sound more dangerous?"

All this may seem like a long way to establish what I already knew.

It is. If I was right.

The value of using questions to confirm my hypothesis becomes evident only when my hypothesis is wrong—which, by the way, is true in my experience about half the time!

Let's suppose that you answered Question 3 differently, by saying, "He has already lied to the giant's wife, after she was so kind to him." In this case, my hypothesis was not exactly correct. Instead of more oomph in the giant, you may need more love and betrayal in Jack's relationship with the giant's wife. By asking questions, however, I have learned what your story really needs before I ever ventured my unhelpful idea about making the giant frightening.

Obviously, the answers to the earlier questions might also surprise me, pointing us to completely different improvements in your story.

A suggestion like "Make the giant scarier" just sits there, based as it is on a single hypothesis.

A series of questions, however, can adapt to flexibly follow each new piece of information about your intentions. As my hypothesis changes, the questions can still lead you to a more effective way of expressing your goals.

For another example of a similar use of questions, see Jerry's session, which follows. (In particular, refer to "Indirect Suggestions: a Series of Questions," page 78.)

When to Give Suggestions

A suggestion is a potent tool. It can provide you with new techniques, possibilities, and solutions. The section of this book, "Coaching to Overcome the Obstacles" (starting on page 89), elaborates the art of using this tool. Like the potentially injurious power of an electric saw, however, the power of a suggestion brings a corresponding risk.

The following coaching session shows some of the potential danger of making suggestions.

JERRY'S STORY

Jerry told a children's story based on a traditional Ozark folksong, "China Doll." In Jerry's adaptation of the song, a child asks her mother for a doll with a porcelain china head, only to be asked, "What will we sell to buy it with?" The child answers the question, only to be faced with more questions:

Child: *We could sell our Daddy's feather bed.*
Mother: *Then where would Daddy sleep?*
Child: *Daddy could sleep in the horse's bed.*
Mother: *Then where would the horse sleep?*

The series of questions and answers continues, ending this way:

Child: *The pigs could play in the front lawn.*

Mother: *Then where would our children play?*
Child: *They could swing on the garden gate.*
Mother: *Yes, and get a licking, too.*

Jerry told his story, while I listened. Then, with his permission, I gave him appreciations. When I asked if he wanted suggestions, he said, "Yes, especially about the ending. I don't like the mother spanking the child; I don't want the mother to win the argument; and it doesn't seem to fit with the rest of the story. Do you have any ideas?"

As it happened, I had a great idea. I knew the song, and knew it was part of a family of folksongs that includes "There's a Hole in the Bucket" and the English "Milking Pails"—songs that generally make a complete circle. (The problem of the hole in the bucket, for example, requires making a patch of wood, which in turn requires cutting the wood, which requires sharpening the saw, which requires water, which requires a trip to the well—but that's impossible, because there's a hole in the bucket.)

My brilliant suggestion was to begin the story with the mother complaining about the child's form of play: "Why are you swinging on the garden gate? Why aren't you playing inside?" Then the child could reply, "Because I need you to buy me a china doll." The final questions could be:

Child: *The pigs could play in the front lawn.*
Mother: *Then where would our children play?*
Child: *They could swing on the garden gate.*
Mother: *Why aren't they playing inside?*
Child: *Because they need you to buy them a china doll!*

This ending eliminates the "licking," gives the child the victory, and fits perfectly with the playful quality of the story.

Should I offer my idea?

OFFERING A DIRECT SUGGESTION FOR JERRY'S STORY

Suppose that I offer my suggestion to Jerry. Let's stop the coaching session at this moment, and imagine Jerry's possible responses.

First, imagine that I offer my idea and that Jerry doesn't like it. In the best case, Jerry would just say, "Naw," and we'd go on. More likely, however, Jerry would feel conflicted. After all, his coach just made a suggestion that seems "off." He wonders whether I misunderstood him, or which of us is actually thinking better about the story. As a result, Jerry has to choose between his own sense of what he wants and his regard for my opinion. If he chooses to reject my idea, he may feel that he is rejecting me. My suggestion has forced him, in a way, to choose between me and his own aesthetics.

For a second possibility, imagine that I offer my great idea and that Jerry *does* like it. He adopts my suggestion and recognizes the brilliance of my thinking. In the best case, of course, Jerry would just feel pleased to have the problem solved, and would learn from this example how to make similar changes in future stories. More likely, however, Jerry would feel another kind of conflict. He has ended up with a great version of the story, but whose version is it? Mine! He may end up feeling dependent on me or distanced from the story. My suggestion has forced him to choose between his love of my idea and his sense of ownership of the story.

Is there another possibility?

Yes—if I do not offer my suggestion directly.

You may want to say, "Wait! Your idea is clearly better than Jerry's, even for achieving his own goals! Shouldn't you just tell him how he could make his story better?"

I respond by describing a still better alternative. If I offer my suggestion more indirectly, I can minimize the danger of forcing Jerry into difficult choices, while still allowing Jerry to benefit from my insight. The indirect suggestion may even make it more likely that Jerry will improve on my insight.

INDIRECT SUGGESTIONS: A SERIES OF QUESTIONS

My first indirect approach is to use my suggestion as the "blueprint" for a series of questions that will allow Jerry to find his own version of "my" ending. I can ask myself, "If my suggestion is an answer, what is the question?"

In this case, I might form the question in my own mind as: "Is there a way to make the story circular?" Then I could say to Jerry, "You know, there are songs that use this question-and-answer structure but end by returning to the first question. I wonder if the story would be even better if you found a way to make the story circle back to the beginning."

If Jerry says, "No, I don't like circular stories," then nothing has been lost. He has rejected the premise of my suggestion, but he never had to confront my actual idea.

Suppose, on the other hand, that Jerry says, "How can I do that?"

I can say, "Where does the story end now?"

"With the licking."

I can reply, "Why is the mother threatening a licking?"

"Because the child is swinging on the garden gate."

I can ask, "What if swinging on the garden gate were in the beginning?"

Jerry might respond with a flood of insight:

"Oh, I get it! The child is swinging on the garden gate because she doesn't have a china doll. So, at the beginning she could say, 'Mommy, I'm bored! I'm going to swing on the garden gate.' Then the mother says, 'Why don't you play inside, instead?' Then the child says, 'Then buy me a china doll.'

"At the end, the child could say, 'The children are bored, so they swing on the garden gate.' Then the initial dialogue repeats and ends with the child asking for the china doll again."

Notice that, if I use questions instead of a suggestion, Jerry may discover an ending similar to mine that he has created himself—but with elements of his own, like the boredom of the children. I provided the idea of a circular story—an abstract idea that he can easily apply to other stories—but I led him to provide the actual ending. In this hypothetical session, he has retained ownership of the story.

INDIRECT SUGGESTIONS: MULTIPLE ALTERNATIVES

My second indirect approach can be used if the first fails. Perhaps Jerry can't understand my questions without an example. In this case, I can challenge myself to provide several examples, not just one.

If Jerry's response to my questions is, "I don't know what you mean by a circular story," I will first try to give examples, such as "The Stonecutter," or "Hole in the Bucket."

If Jerry still does not understand, I may need to give further examples using Jerry's story:

> To make this story circular, make the ending return to the beginning. For example, you could have the story end by coming back to what the child wanted: the china doll, or not to be bored, or to have the mother finally buy something for *her.*
>
> Or you could change the beginning to match the ending: the child was threatened with a licking at the start, or was caught swinging on the garden gate, or needs to be allowed to play outside the front yard.

In giving Jerry these concrete ideas, I purposely gave multiple examples. I gave two basic ideas: change the ending or change the beginning. For each of the two basic ideas, I came up with three separate thoughts. (E.g., "the china doll, or not to be bored, or to have the mother finally buy something for her.")

This way, no single suggestion carries all the weight of my authority. Jerry is not faced with accepting or rejecting the only possibility, but with choosing one of several. Responding to a few different suggestions, he is more likely to create a hybrid of his own.

IS THIS INDIRECTNESS NECESSARY?

One might ask, "Isn't all this indirectness in giving suggestions just a way of coddling the storyteller? Wouldn't it be better to just make the suggestion outright, then expect the storyteller to deal with any feelings it brings up? We need the efficiency of giving bald suggestions."

To be sure, it is possible to obscure a simple insight with a flurry of unnecessary "niceness." If the goals and time are very limited, it may be reasonable to say, "Here's how I would do it. Decide for yourself."

All the same, it is tempting for the coach to overlook the negative effects of these direct suggestions. Even the best coach can misconstrue the storyteller's intention. When that happens, the coach's suggestions may further obscure the storyteller's true intentions, thus actually slowing the story's progress toward full realization. Further, such externally-provided suggestions may slow the storyteller's progress toward realizing her independent creativity.

Thus, it is usually more efficient to be indirect.

Jerry's actual session went differently from the hypothetical sessions just described. After hearing that he was dissatisfied with his original ending, I asked him the question, "What if you found a way to make the story circular?" Of course, I expected him to either reject the idea or to make the story circular by coming up with a beginning similar to mine.

Jerry surprised me. He said, "I get it! I'll change the ending to bring back the china doll. The child will answer the last question, 'Then where would our children play?' by saying, 'They'd be playing with the china doll!' "

He didn't change the beginning to match the ending (as I had proposed); he just changed the ending. Not only did he come up with an ending that he had created himself, he came up with a better one than I had thought of.

Avoiding direct suggestions can also be a way of showing my belief in you. I take the extra trouble to turn my idea into a series of questions or multiple suggestions because, by respecting you in this way, I may further unleash your creativity. I assume not only that you can succeed, but that you can succeed in ways that will astonish me.

What Else Would You Like?

When I listen to you as your coach, I help draw out of you the uniqueness of your storytelling (or of your approach to achieving responsible fiscal management). When I give you appreciations, I offer you important information about what already succeeds in your storytelling or project. When I give you suggestions, I offer you information about where you are not succeeding and about possible ways to improve. What else might you need?

I don't know what else you need. I have to ask you.

To learn what else you need, I can devote the final part of the four-part structure to whatever goals of yours remain unmet. This fourth part begins when I ask, "What else would you like from me?"

Typically, you will respond in one of three ways. Sometimes, you will say, "No, that's all." In this case, I accomplish nothing remarkable in this section, but you and I are both reminded that your goals are primary in the coaching process.

Other times, you will ask for more appreciation. You might say, "Nothing more, I guess. But do you think the story is OK?" Or else: "How about the wedding scene? Did that work for people?"

In this case, it is time for me to add or reiterate appropriate appreciations. You are saying, in effect, "I need to hear a specific appreciation that I didn't yet hear," or "I need to hear an appreciation again." As in the appreciation period, you may need specific or general appreciation, or appreciation about you, the story, or your effect on the audience. By listening carefully to the request, I can often know what kind of appreciation to give.

By the way, it may seem that your question, "Did that work for people?" is a request for evaluation. In fact, it may be. But it is more prudent for me to treat it first as a request for appreciation. After more appreciations, I can ask again, "Is there anything else you'd like from us?" When I give you an extra appreciation, I do no harm, but when I give you an unsought suggestion or evaluation I run slightly more risk of discouraging or disempowering you.

Still other times, you will respond by asking for help with a new subject. For example, you may ask, "I may want to tell that story for an adult audience, as well as for the child audiences I described to you. Do you think it will work?"

When you make such a request, it usually makes sense for me to recapitulate the four-part structure in miniature: first, I listen carefully to your request; then I give appreciations of the story as a story for adults; then I give suggestions; finally, I ask if anything else is needed to meet your request.

Before ending your coaching session, I usually repeat an appreciation or two. In addition, I often point you toward your future success or your likely lasting impact upon me:

- You have a wonderful way of telling. I hope you keep it up.
- The character of the mother is unforgettable. I can't wait to hear how that story develops!
- The moment when you opened the package was so vivid. I won't soon forget it!
- You gave me a new understanding of what it's like to be a single mother. I think the world needs to hear more of that point of view.

Such appreciations leave you with a reminder of what went well—just in case you forgot it in the course of hearing suggestions. It is also a final chance for me to express the fundamental principle of coaching: my belief in your success.

Managing the Four-Part Structure

The coach needs to adapt the four-part structure to meet the unique needs of each presenter. Coaching in a third-grade classroom, for example, will need to be managed differently from coaching in a board room or adult church retreat. Group coaching will require different procedures from individual coaching.

In most cases, you will feel more in charge—and therefore

safer and more willing to experiment—if I first explain my principles, if I ask your permission before beginning each part of our work together, and if I take charge of guiding any others present.

EXPLAINING THE PRINCIPLES

When I begin by explaining the principles of coaching, I distinguish this coaching session from other helping encounters—beneficial or otherwise—you have had in the past.

By explaining the coaching principles as I see them, I describe how I understand my role. This frees you to accept, question, or renegotiate any part of my proposed role as coach. As a result, we can agree to a tacit contract.

How do I explain the principles of coaching? The best explanation will be adapted to the situation at hand. It may range from, "I'm here to help you get better at this," to a detailed description of the principles, ground rules and four-part structure. I describe what I believe, in my own words, in a way that is appropriate for my listeners.

If I explain my role with respect and warmth, I am already increasing your emotional safety and starting to put you in charge.

ASKING PERMISSION

At each stage of the four-part structure, I ask your permission before proceeding. This is another use of questions. (See "Kinds of Suggestions #3," page 72.) In all cases, these questions are only likely to be helpful if spoken with a genuine tone of respect. (See "Toning Up Our Praise," page 61.)

Before I begin listening to your presentation, I ask you, "Would you like to start now?" I may add other questions, such as:

- Do you need anything else before you start?
- Where would you like to be in the room?
- Where would you like us to be?
- Do you have any special instructions for us as listeners?

This might also be a good time for me to ask about any specific needs I think you might have:

- Would you like to be tape recorded?
- Do you need a glass of water?
- Will it distract you if I take notes while you speak?

If, after listening, I intend to go on to give appreciations, I ask your permission again: "Would you like to hear appreciations?" Of course, I ask this question in a form that makes sense given the situation:

- Would you like to hear what people liked about your story?
- I made a list of things I especially liked. Are you ready for it?

If, after giving appreciations, I think it makes sense to go on to give suggestions, I ask your permission yet again:

- Would you like to hear some thoughts about how to make your story even better?
- Can I have a turn with suggestions?
- Would you like people's reactions to parts that could be better?

If, during suggestions, I hope to try something that might work better without being explained in advance, I can ask your permission to begin an unspecified activity:

- Are you willing to try something?
- I have an idea for another way to approach this. Are you game to try it?
- Do you want to try an exercise to help with this?

Usually, after suggestions, I will ask what else you would like from me or the group.

- I may also ask your permission before ending each section:
- Can we end appreciations now?
- How about taking two more appreciations before we stop?
- Would it be all right to finish suggestions at this point?
- Is this a good place to stop?
- Can we end now?

Of course, if our "contract" includes time constraints, I will honor them as respectfully as possible:

- We have just three more minutes. Would you like more appreciations, or would you like a suggestion?

- We are nearly out of time. Is there anything else you'd like from us?

When time is really up, it might make sense for me to learn if you have unmet needs, even when I do not have the opportunity to meet them immediately:

- We need to stop now. Did we leave you in a good place?
- Someone else needs this room now. If we left something unfinished, would you please call or write me about it?

When I ask you any of these questions, I do not assume consent. If I detect any reluctance in your answer, I pause. I may repeat the question. I remind you, "It is your choice!" I proceed only when I feel sure that you have actually given your permission.

TAKING CHARGE OF THE GROUP

When I coach you in a group setting, I am also training the group as assistant coaches. Their listening, appreciations, and suggestions can greatly augment my own.

Not only do the other participants add value to your session, they receive value from it, too. They may gain as much as storytellers (or as dentists or as layout artists) from watching me coach you as they would gain from being coached themselves.

If I fail to take charge of their contributions, however, an untrained group can obstruct your goals.

My explanation of principles and my asking your permission are doubly important in group coaching, because they serve to educate the group about the goals for the coaching session and about the need to keep you in charge of the process.

Sometimes, I will add ground rules expressly for the group setting.

When I ask a group of listeners to give you appreciations or suggestions, for example, I usually ask them to raise their hands before speaking. Then I explain that, since the coaching is for your sake, you should be in charge of who speaks and when. If *you* call on group members for their contributions, not only will you hear the contribution you want to hear at that moment, but you will also be in charge of the flow—of the rate at which contributions come to you. This control will allow you to finish dealing with one contribution before going on to the next. Further, group members will be encouraged to direct their comments to you, not to me.

Frequently, in their eagerness to help (or to achieve a less beneficial goal, such as to prove themselves right or to establish your deviation from perfection), the group will fail to notice that your agenda is no longer being met. I can assist you at such moments by interrupting them, saying, "Notice what's happening! The storyteller is still thinking about the last comment, while we're waving our hands, trying to get her attention. I suggest we put our hands down and watch her eyes to know when she is ready for more input. She'll probably look at us when she's done thinking."

Another group behavior that I interrupt immediately is cross-talk. Eager to solve your problem for you or to respond to each other's comments, group members may start talking to each other instead of to you. One may say to another, "But your suggestion is unnecessary if the storyteller takes my earlier suggestion ...."

I usually say, "Hold on! Here's a common pitfall for us as coaches. Do you see how we've started to talk to each other? It's tempting, isn't it? I think we should direct all our comments to the storyteller. Our goal is to assist her in solving her problems—which is different from solving them ourselves."

Often, our allotted time will end before you have heard every group member's contribution. I can help you stay in charge after the session by warning the group in advance of the third ground rule ("I Won't Refer to Your Prior Sessions Without Your Permission," page 44).

Occasionally, the group members have such a strong need to be heard that they are temporarily unable to listen to you well. In this case, I have the option of stopping your coaching session momentarily in order to try to meet their needs before continuing. I might say something like this:

"We're taking a time-out from the storyteller's coaching session. Get a partner to talk to. One of you will listen without interrupting for three minutes while the other one talks about whatever you need to talk about. When I call 'switch,' the other person will talk for three minutes. Go!"

If I wish, I can also give one or all of the group members a chance to speak (usually more briefly) in front of the group: "Now that you've each spoken to a partner, I'd like to hear you tell me thirty seconds of what's on your mind." Once some of their need to talk has been met, we can resume your coaching session.

DISCARDING THE WHOLE STRUCTURE

The four-part structure is designed to help you. Many times, it will. When it would be more helpful not to use it, however, I jettison it.

About thirty-three percent of the time, I modify the four-part structure to adapt to a particular presenter's needs. Another ten percent of the time, I ignore it completely, substituting some other way to help the storyteller.

Standard eating utensils are valuable tools. Still, if a straw meets your needs better, I should not insist on giving you a knife, fork and spoon.

Your coaching session is for your benefit. The four-part structure is a powerful tool that—sometimes—can help meet your needs.

Coaching to Overcome The First Obstacle: Lack of Information

Coaching to Overcome the Obstacles

As your coach, I believe in the possibility of your success. If your story (or your speech, grant application, or collage) is not succeeding at the moment, however, what then?

Some obstacle must be temporarily preventing your success.

My job is to help you overcome the obstacle.

I need to understand your obstacle. I need to see how it differs from other obstacles as well as how it resembles them. I need a repertoire of general strategies for your type of obstacle that I can then customize for your unique situation.

This section describes the four principle kinds of obstacles, and the kinds of tools available to me to help you overcome them.

The Categories of Obstacles

Since you are unique, you encounter unique obstacles. Nonetheless, your unique obstacle will fall into a common category. Each different category of obstacles requires a different category of help.

ANALOGY: CALLING UP A FRIEND

Suppose you want to talk to a particular new acquaintance. This is your goal—which, of course, I believe you are capable of achieving. Therefore, when I learn that you have not succeeded in talking to this acquaintance, I conclude that an obstacle has presented itself.

What is your obstacle? There are an infinite number of potential obstacles, but they fall into four categories.

Suppose you just don't know your new acquaintance's phone number. In this case you need information. You need the phone number. Or a phone directory. Of course, there many other kinds of information you could need. Maybe you don't know his area code. Maybe you don't even know how to use the telephone.

This first kind of obstacle includes the need for information in the broadest sense, whether contained in a simple fact, a detailed briefing, or a graduate program full of learning. You may need information about how to communicate, about what you want to communicate, or about your listeners.

Suppose, however, that you know your new acquaintance's number, but you just don't know what you want to say to him. If you actually dial the phone and he answers, you are stumped. You can't form a coherent sentence. In this case, you may need to explore what it is that you actually want to communicate to him. Or you may need to imagine your intended communication in more detail, so that you can put your intention into words. You need more experience of your message.

This second kind of obstacle includes gaining clarity about what you want to say, through understanding your intention or through imagining your message more fully.

Consider a third possibility. What if there is an easier way to reach your acquaintance than the way you are trying? Suppose you have assumed that he has a phone, but he doesn't? In this case, the best way to reach him may be to find his address. To overcome this third type of obstacle, you first have to stop looking for his phone number. Only then can you begin looking for his address. This is the kind of obstacle I call misdirected effort.

Any false assumption can lead you into misdirected effort—putting your energy where it hinders rather than helps.

There is one more category of obstacle. Suppose you are afraid of your new acquaintance—even though you have every reason to believe he would do you no harm. Your irrational fear is preventing you from talking to him. In this case, you have an emotional block interfering with achieving your goal. Of course, the emotion involved could just as easily be anger, grief, or embarrassment.

HELPING YOU CALL YOUR FRIEND

To help you achieve your goal of talking to your new acquaintance, first I must to establish the kind of obstacle in your way. Then it will be easier for me to determine the appropriate kind of help.

If you need information, I can just tell you his phone number.

If you need more experience of your message, in contrast, I may need to help you explore your intentions or how to express them.

If you are misdirecting effort, I may need to get you to notice that you are busily exploring a dead end, before you can redirect your effort more profitably.

Finally, if you have an emotional block, I need to help you with the feeling itself.

What helps you with one category of obstacle may be irrelevant or even harmful for another. When all you lack is his phone number, it would be silly for me to ask about what you want to say, or to start seeking the content of your fears. But if you need more experience of your message, a phone directory won't help. And if you are truly afraid of calling him, even a six-foot poster with his phone number on it won't enable you to call him.

The First Obstacle

The first obstacle, the need for information, is widely acknowledged. Schools, for example, commonly take the imparting of information as their chief mission. Broadcast media, periodicals, and libraries compete to satisfy our appetite for news and other information. In short, we recognize in our society that people sometimes need to know facts, figures, descriptions, history, theories, or ways of thinking about a subject. As a result, no one is surprised that a coach's role may include the giving of information in its broadest sense.

The need for information is so familiar that we sometimes think we need information when we actually need a different form of assistance. Thus, the very familiarity of the need for information can lead to special dangers for the coach. A request for information can disguise a more fundamental but less recognized need.

To help you efficiently when you need information, I need to be aware of the kind of information you might need, of how to relate the information to your goals, of how to give it to you in a helpful form, and of the circumstances when giving you information might not be helpful at all.

What Kinds of Information Do Storytellers Need?

Unlike the other kinds of obstacles, the need for information is usually specific to the subject matter of your project. An engineer making a progress report needs different information from that needed by a pitcher learning to control a curve ball.

As a storyteller, for example, you may need basic information about storytelling, information about the content or delivery of your story, or information about interacting with your audiences.

As a coach, therefore, it helps me to be aware of the kinds of information you are likely to need.

BASIC INFORMATION ABOUT STORYTELLING

Storytellers often need basic information about oral presentation. You may say, "I can't tell you a story, because I have no idea about how to tell one." In this case, I can be most helpful by giving you the basic information you need. I may talk to you about imagining the scenes of the story in your mind, about creating an outline to help order the scenes, or about telling your story to several individuals to learn and improve it.

If you are more advanced as a storyteller, you may be struggling with a choice of repertoire or with discovering your own style. In this case, I can give you information about the types of stories that exist or about the range of possible styles. I may also help you by talking about the uniqueness of individual styles: all great storytellers tell in their own ways, giving expression—subtle or obvious—to their unique points of view. This information may free you to pursue your own natural style.

THE CONTENT OF YOUR STORY

You may need information specific to the particular story you are telling.

You may need background information. If you are struggling to tell your version of the Romeo and Juliet story, set in colonial America, you may need information about the historical setting you have chosen for your story. Or if your "Romeo" and "Juliet" are packets of electronic messages trying to join together on a computer network with feuding protocols, you may need information about computers.

You may need information about the genre of your story.

If you are new to boardroom presentations, for example, you may need to know what the usual expectations are for stories told within such presentations and any particular expectations within the corporation for whom you are presenting. If, on the other hand, you are telling a campfire ghost story to teenagers, you may need to know this audience's—quite different—expectations.

You may need information about any specialized component of your storytelling. If your boardroom presentation includes a demonstration of a new product, you need to know about the product and how to use it. If your story for young children includes a string figure, you need to know how to create and display it.

THE DELIVERY OF YOUR STORY

You may need information about how to deliver your story. You may need to know ways to portray characters through posture and voice, or ways to simulate conversation between two characters. You may need information about vocal projection or about how to use pauses effectively.

If you are accompanying your boardroom story with a slide show, you need to know how to operate the slide projector. If you are using a flannel board to tell stories to young children, you need to know how to manipulate the flannel shapes without losing your connection to your audience.

INTERACTION WITH YOUR AUDIENCE

Finally, you may need information about interacting with your audience.

You may need information about maintaining eye contact with a large group, or about adapting the size of your gestures for different size groups.

You may need to know how you can involve your audience in active participation, using techniques like asking questions or singing or acting out roles in a story.

You may need information about dealing with disruptive audience members or with eager but noisy listeners.

WHEN YOU NEED INFORMATION THAT I DON'T HAVE

As the preceding list of topics illustrates, helping you overcome lack of information can make substantial demands on my store of knowledge. If I don't have certain information, I can't give it to you.

It will not help you for me to pretend to have information that I do not have.

When I don't know something, I can still be helpful by identifying what you need to know, and then acknowledging that I don't know it.

Sometimes, I can help further by referring you to other

sources for the information.

TEACHING ME WHAT YOU NEED TO KNOW

Still other times—surprisingly often—I can learn the information you need *from you*. This is possible when your success is inconsistent. By noticing how you are succeeding and explaining your own unconscious techniques to you, I can help you succeed more consistently.

Eileen told a personal story in a coaching workshop about an embarrassing day as a bridesmaid on a shipboard wedding. The climax of her story came when she hopped ashore—carefully dressed down to a corsage on her wrist—and pushed the boat from the dock. In the process, she found herself stretched between the dock and the boat; unable to correct her balance, she fell into Boston harbor.

As Eileen told this section of her story, she reached out her arms, imitating how she had pushed the boat. As she described the boat getting farther from the dock, she leaned farther and farther forward.

Even though this section of the story was funny, there was something about her telling of it that didn't seem as funny as it should have been. The humor was present, but not sustained.

As a coach, of course, I believed that Eileen was capable of achieving her goal by sharing the humor in this experience. Since she was not succeeding entirely, I knew there must be an obstacle in her way.

It occurred to me that Eileen might have been unaware of how she created her humorous effects. This prevented her from following through consistently. So I needed to notice what she was doing right, and then explain it to her. She needed information about how she made things funny!

I noticed that her physical action of leaning forward created a tension, contrasting with her chatty talk about doubling as bridesmaid and first mate. I realized that humor can depend on opposition and contrast; in this case, the contrast was between her imminent physical danger and her casual talk. As she told the story, she stopped leaning forward at one point—and that was where the humorous tension had dissipated.

I explained all this to her, then asked her to try the scene again while remaining aware of the physical aspect of the tension. When the retelling made me and the other workshop members laugh throughout, I knew I had correctly identified the obstacle. Further, I had learned the information she needed, and given it back to her in a form that she could use.

Relating Information To Your Goals

Whatever kind of information you need, you will learn it most easily if it interests you. Before you will be interested in any information, you need to understand how it relates to what you want to do. Therefore, I help you best when I can relate new information to your established goals.

Natalie told a story for children, a version of "The Gingerbread Man." Her runaway Gingerbread Man met character after character, bragging to each about all the other characters he had outrun. Whenever he met a new character, he sang, to the tune of "Hot Cross Buns,"

Gingerbread Man!
Gingerbread Man!
I am the tasty
Gingerbread Man!

As I listened, I felt that the song added little to the story. It didn't push the plot along, it wasn't much fun to sing, and it seemed too "goody-goody" to fit the slightly saucy character of her Gingerbread Man.

As a coach, I might have stated my reaction, saying, "The song isn't as much fun as it could be." Or I might have made a general suggestion, "How about improving the song?" Ideally, I would make a more specific suggestion, along the lines of "How about making the song have more of the quality of ...."

But I didn't know what quality the song should have.

Therefore, I needed to know more about her goals in the story. I asked her about them:

Coach: *What do you love about the story?*
Natalie: *I love the Gingerbread Man.*
Coach: *Tell me more.*
Natalie: *He's just not afraid of anybody. He's out to see the world, and he won't let anyone stop him.*

Having learned her goals, I could now help her change the song so that it would further them:

Coach: *Could you put his fearless attitude into the song?*
Natalie: *Sure, I want to. How do I do that?*

If Natalie had been conversant with adapting or creating songs, she would have been able to change the song on her own, and my job would have been done. But she needed information in order to express her character's spunk through song.

I taught her how to start with a physical attitude for her character—in her case, she chose a swagger. Then, walking as her character would walk, I had her begin to chant what her character would say. After a few attempts, she said, "Watch out, world, here I come!" Everyone in the workshop recognized the vitality in that phrase as she said it. With more information and guidance from me, she ended up with a four-line "rap" that conveyed some of her character's cheekiness and determination:

Watch out, world, here I come!
I'm the Gingerbread Man and I'm on the run.
I want to travel, won't be denied,
Watch out, world! Step aside!

If I had not known how to create songs, I could still have referred Natalie to another source: a person, a book, or examples of other songs and stories. Since Natalie now had a reason for wanting to learn this information, she might have learned it even if I could not teach it.

In this session, I had done several things. First, I had noticed my own reaction to her song. Then I established Natalie's goals in the story, and suggested she change the song to help achieve them. At this point, I discovered that her obstacle was needing information about creating songs to express character. When I presented the information, therefore, it was in the context of her goals. Although she was frightened about creating songs, she knew that the information was relevant to her.

Finally, I gave the information in a hands-on fashion, which seemed to suit her learning style. This leads us to another topic: I always need to present information in a style that suits you.

Let's Do It Your Way

When I attended school, most teachers presented a given piece of information in only one way. Some of us understood, others did not. No one expected the teacher to change her presentation based on our individual learning styles.

To be most effective, I will do what my own teachers seldom did: vary the style of teaching to fit your favored modes of learning.

To do this, I need to be aware that I can explain things in different ways. In fact, explanation itself is only one of my tools for giving information.

When I offer you information, I need to give it in whatever form you can understand. It is my job to keep trying different ways until I finally allow you to succeed.

✧ THE TEACHER'S ANGER ✧

One Wednesday in September, I found myself sitting around a table with five other adult students and Hungarian master teacher Lenci Horvath. We were the complete student body of the academic year class at the Kodály Musical Training Institute. We would be together six hours a day, five days a week, for nine months.

All of us trusted Lenci already, having studied with her in summer courses.

But we weren't so sure about each other. None of us

wanted to be with students who were too far ahead of us, or too far behind us. We didn't want to be held back or to feel inferior.

This was the third day of class. Sometime mid-morning, Lenci called on Dorothy to sing a simple passage. When Dorothy came to the sequence of notes "do-mi," she faltered. Lenci asked her to sing "do-mi" by itself; Dorothy did so, easily. Then Lenci asked Dorothy to repeat the whole passage. Dorothy made the same mistake again!

Now Lenci came up with another way to assist Dorothy. She suggested, "Sing the note that is between the other two, as well." Dorothy sang, "Do-re-mi." Lenci said, "Now just imagine the middle note, 're.' " Dorothy did it perfectly. But when she tried the passage again, she faltered just as before.

By now, the rest of us were exchanging impatient looks. We were all frustrated with Dorothy's shortcomings. This was clearly going to be a long year.

Lenci, however, remained perfectly calm and encouraging. She said, "Remember the song we learned yesterday that has the opening notes, do-mi? Sing the words of that song. Good! Now sing those words when you get to the 'do-mi' in our passage. Good! Now sing the passage normally." In spite of all this help from Lenci, Dorothy missang yet again.

We students were glaring at Dorothy. What a dolt! She clearly did not belong here.

Finally, Lenci's tone changed. She was getting frustrated, too. She remained silent for a long moment. We braced ourselves for the imminent tirade at Dorothy's ineptness.

Then Lenci spoke. "There must be *some* way I can help you with this!"

Whoa! I did a double-take.

Lenci was frustrated, but not with Dorothy. She was angry at her own inability to teach!

First I felt sheepish. I had completely misunderstood

Lenci's attitude.

Then relief washed over me like a soothing bath. If Lenci kept trying until all of us would learn, then I didn't have to make sure I was good enough to be in the class. She would help me wherever I was. We could each learn in whatever way we needed to learn. Lenci held herself responsible for finding that way.

With meek grins at each other, the six of us settled down to learn together.

SEARCHING FOR HOW TO GIVE INFORMATION

Jason told a beautiful story about his childhood relationship with his grandfather. In telling it, however, he tended to "telegraph" by telling us before each scene what conclusion we were to draw from it:

"I really liked my grandfather. Every day after school, I snuck over to his apartment for a heart-to-heart talk ...."

Or:

"One day I got really frightened. I woke up, got out of bed, and there was no one in the house. I just had a feeling there was something wrong ...."

Or:

"My grandfather always made me feel safe. One day, the local bully came over to our street and ...."

The first sentence in each of these paragraphs is unnecessary. By telling us that he snuck over to his grandfather's apartment every day, for example, we learn that Jason really liked his grandfather; it's superfluous to tell us in advance.

Of course, only Jason can decide whether to retain these sentences. But before he can do that, I had to explain to him what they were. I had to give him information. I began by giving an abstract definition:

To "telegraph" is to tell us the content or the meaning of a scene before it happens.

Some people are perfectly at home with this kind of definition, and would immediately understand what I meant. Jason responded by looking blank, however, so I went on to add an example or two (from the samples given above).

Many people, given two or three examples, would respond by stating back the information in their own words, such as, "Oh, you mean I don't need a topic sentence for each paragraph, right?" At this point, the information would have been received.

GOING BEYOND DEFINITIONS AND EXAMPLES

In Jason's case, however, my examples did not make my point clear. To make sure, I asked, "Is that clear at all?" When he shook his head, I went on to try a different form of explanation—through imagery or analogy:

In an instructional film on keeping your child from being kidnapped, you'd see a title on the screen or hear a narrator saying, "Beware of dangerous strangers!"

But in an dramatic film about a kidnapping, you'd just see the stranger walking down the street. She might check her map to see where to go; that's how you'd know she is a stranger. Maybe she'd open her purse and load her gun; that's how you'd know she is dangerous.

The titles or the narrator in the instructional film "telegraph" what's coming. But in a story you don't need to. You can just go right into the adventure.

So far, I had tried an abstract definition, then had given examples, then had given him a chance to state back the idea in his own words, and then used an analogy. When Jason let me know that I still hadn't hit the mark, I tried another method, the "hands-on" approach.

I asked Jason to tell a scene from his story, so I could point out "telegraphing" as it happened. He began, "The rest of my family didn't really like Grandpa. You see, ..."

I stopped him immediately, saying, "Why did you tell us that the rest of the family didn't like him?"

Jason said, "I was just reminding myself what came next."

I said, "What I call 'telegraphing' is saying the parts where you remind yourself what comes next." He nodded in understanding. Only then did I continue, "My suggestion is to just think those parts where you remind yourself what's coming, without saying them aloud."

Jason had received the information. It did not matter at all how many attempts had failed along the way. I had succeeded.

Other Ways to Customize Information

The method that worked in explaining this idea to Jason was first for him to do what I was trying to explain, then for me to call his attention to it, and finally for him to describe it in his own words.

In addition to the different forms of explanation that I tried, I could also have searched for the sensory mode that is most comfortable for Jason. Some people prefer visual descriptions, whereas others respond more easily to auditory or kinesthetic (muscular) imagery. When I described the film analogy for Jason, for example, I might have also given other analogies that used sound (a radio program where the announcer always tells the titles before playing the songs) or movement (a baseball pitcher who always looks to the right before throwing a pitch outside).

The Information Framework

A powerful form of information is what I call a "framework." A framework sets forth a principle and its opposite, allowing you to evaluate your options in terms of gains and losses, pros and cons. It helps you use information to make choices of your own.

Does Audrey Need Information?

Audrey told a traditional folktale she had adapted. After hearing appreciations, she said, "I want to know if it's OK to change a folktale as much as I did."

On the surface, Audrey appeared to request information: a "yes" or a "no." On closer inspection, however, it is clear that Audrey actually asked for validation of her choice.

This is always a dangerous moment for the coach. Whether I say, "Yes, it's OK," or "No, it's not OK," I usurp Audrey's decision-making powers.

Instead, I want to help Audrey make the decision that best suits her own purposes.

To help Audrey make a better-informed decision, I can give her a framework within which she can make the decision herself. This framework is a form of information—but not the "yes" or "no" information she requested. It presents the pros and cons of changes to traditional stories. Using it, Audrey can assess the effects of her changes to the story.

A Framework for Adapting Traditional Stories

I told Audrey that tellers of traditional stories have two masters to serve. One master is tradition. After all, a folktale has survived because generations of people found it important enough to preserve in their hearts. The folktale arose from the deep well of a culture and contains within it some part of that culture's experience and wisdom. To serve this master, the storyteller must keep the ancient qualities intact.

At the same time, the teller serves another master: the requirements of the present moment—the need to bring the story to life right here, right now. If, in my desire to serve the master of tradition, I tell the story in a form that cannot be comprehended by my listeners, nothing will be passed on. I will have failed both masters!

Similarly, if I make the story appeal to my audience by changing it beyond recognition, I may have sacrificed that which made the tale worth telling. My current audience will be deprived of the tale's deep appeal. Again, I have cheated the master of the present moment as well as the master of tradition.

Therefore, to serve either master well, I must keep them both in mind at all times. I must seek and preserve as much as possible of the tale's deep meanings, while still telling it in a way that delights my audience. To decide about the validity of any change to the tale, I can ask myself, "Is this change preserving the essence of the tradition? Is it also allowing this essence to live in the present?"

This framework may not be the final word on the controversial issue of folktale adaptations, but it was a way for me to give information that still allowed Audrey to make her own decision. When she retells the folktale a year from now, she can make a new decision based on the same framework. I have made her less dependent on my judgment, not more so.

FROM OPINION TO FRAMEWORK

When you ask me how to make a decision about an issue, my first response is often to think how I would decide the same issue. If I just tell you this first response, it may help you in some way. At least you will learn one opinion that could be held.

I can help you more, though, if I can generalize from my personal decision or opinion to create a framework that will encompass other possible opinions as well.

Suppose you ask whether to use puppets in a particular story. Suppose also that my first thought is, "No! Don't bring puppets near that story!"

To create a framework from this reaction, I need first to notice what information my reaction is based on. Exploring my own reaction, I notice, "I don't want the puppets in that story because they seem to limit the story for me. I was enjoying the images I had created of the characters, and the puppets seem dull by comparison." Now I have learned something about the problem: puppets replace my images with something less appealing. I'm making progress toward creating a framework!

Next, I need to discover the opposing principle. What good could puppets possibly be?

Since I believe in the diversity of success (see the "Coaching Principles" chapter), I know that people can succeed in ways very different from my own way. Even if I hate puppets, therefore, I believe that it is at least theoretically possible to use them in ways that can transform an audience. (In fact, I have seen transcendent artistry using puppets, but I could create a framework about puppets even if I had not.) How could I, as a puppet nonbeliever, describe the advantages of using puppets?

The key may lie in the very reaction I had against puppets. They substituted an external visual image for my cherished internal one. Under what circumstances would that external image be an advantage? Some audiences, I realize, might have difficulty creating their own images, especially at the start. They might be young, inexperienced with imagery, or in a distracting environment. In fact, some audiences may be able to create even more imaginative and splendid internal images while looking at the puppets than while looking at the storyteller.

So what is the principle here? Puppets provide an external, visual stimulus that gives more variety than a storyteller's body does. That's the advantage. The disadvantage is that the listener's internal images can be overpowered by the physical reality of the puppets. There's my framework, as it emerged from my personal opinion.

Of course, there are other possible advantages to puppets. It's not required that I know them all, only that I figure out the ones that are relevant to your impulse to use puppets. To be sure that I have understood the relevant advantages, I can ask you why you thought of using puppets for this story. If your answer fits in my framework (e.g., "I tell to two-year-olds, and they seem to like looking at the puppets"), then I can use my framework to help you see the trade-offs and make your own decision.

If your answer does not fit in my framework, however, then I need to change or expand the framework. Suppose you say, "I like to make the different voices." Uh, oh! I hadn't thought about sound. Now why would anyone use puppets for that purpose? I'd better ask. So I say, "Tell me more."

If you now say, "I feel more comfortable making crazy voices when I use puppets," then I can expand my framework. Now I realize that puppets can also have the advantage of freeing the storyteller from the inhibiting scrutiny of the audience—and they have the corresponding disadvantage of reducing the teller's direct contact with the audience. Again, I can present both sides in a framework that allows you to make an informed choice.

When I Should Not Give Information

Even when your obstacle is lack of information, there are times when it does not make sense for me to try to give you information. Such times are when I'm not ready to give, when you are not ready to receive, or when there is a question about which information you actually need.

WHEN I'M NOT READY TO GIVE

Sometimes you need information, but I'm not ready to give it to you. Ideally, I will notice that I'm not ready before I start.

I may not know what you need to know. (See "When You Need Information that I Don't Have," page 94.)

I may not have thought about the information before, or have worked out a way to explain it clearly. In this case, I may try explaining it first to someone else. In a workshop setting I sometimes call a ten-minute break. During the break, I ask a workshop member to listen while I think aloud about the subject you need to know.

My feelings are a common reason that I'm not ready to give you information. For example, I may notice that I'm feeling annoyed at you for needing this information. I may feel superior to you because I have this information and you don't. Or I may feel pulled to give you advice rather than to lay information at your feet.

When I stop to reflect in any of these cases, I may realize that I have feelings that do not actually relate to you.

My feelings may stem from being tired. I may have given the same piece of information many times recently. I may be trying to attend to you without giving myself the breaks that I need. (See "Dealing With My Needs as Coach," page 53.)

My feelings may also have to do with feeling inadequate. I may have tried unsuccessfully to impart this same information to others, or I may feel that I don't understand it as well as I "should."

My feelings may relate to the information itself. Perhaps I am telling you about your story's background of anti-Semitism, sexism, or racism, for example, and have not yet dealt with my own feelings about being either a victim or a victimizer.

In these cases, it is usually not helpful for me to forge ahead. It may be better to call a time-out while I deal with my feelings, or even to suggest that you get the information elsewhere—including from other people (such as workshop members) who may be present.

When I feel ready to give you the information in a matter-of-fact but encouraging tone of voice, I have probably processed the feelings enough for the moment.

When You're Not Ready to Receive

You are not ready to receive information if you are "full," if you are thinking about something else, or if you do not yet perceive how the information relates to your goals.

In my eagerness to help you, I may have already given you enough to think about for one day. Even though the information addresses a real need of yours, I will help you more by waiting or by just noting that the subject may interest you in the future.

Sometimes, you will have absorbed all you can in one session, but will ask for still more. If I suspect that you are, in fact, already full, I can tell you my perceptions, then let you decide how to proceed.

I can notice that you are not ready for more information if I pay attention to your verbal and non-verbal communication. Your eyes, your stance, your words may tell me whether you are eager or reluctant.

Often you are reluctant to absorb new information because you are thinking of something else. You may still be processing the previous thought, or coming to an important realization about your project.

Still other times, you are slow to embrace my information because you do not yet see how it connects to your goals.

In this case, I need to establish the connection for you or else not give the information. If I cannot convince you that certain information is essential to your goals, it may not be! I may even be confusing your goals with mine.

If you truly need this information, then you'll realize it another day. When that happens, you'll seek the information out and absorb it readily. Until then, you will absorb little of what I say.

✧ The Giant in the Sky ✧

Jean Piaget, the Swiss psychologist, spent a lifetime studying the development of thinking in children. He devised many ingenious ways to determine children's actual, often erroneous, concepts of the world around them.

Early in his career, the story goes, he asked a bright youngster how a nearby mountain range had originated. Piaget dutifully took notes as the child related a quite imaginative tale about how a giant had been playing in a sandbox in the sky, but dumped those huge lumps of earth over the edge, where they still lie.

Having completed his interview of the child, Piaget could not help offering to set the child straight. "That is a wonderful story," he said. "Now, would you like to hear how it really happened?" He went on to explain the dramatic shifting of the earth's crust over many centuries. The child seemed very interested, and even repeated Piaget's explanation back to him.

Some months later, Piaget saw the child again. He asked the youngster, "Do you happen to remember what I told you about how the mountain was really created?"

"Oh, yes," the child responded with enthusiasm. "You told me how one day, a giant was playing in a sandbox in the sky ...."

That was how Piaget learned the futility of giving unsought information.

WHEN THE INFORMATION MAY NOT BE WHAT YOU NEED

Since the need for information is one of the few accepted needs in our society, it usually feels safer for you to ask for information than to ask for other forms of help. In fact, you may not even understand what other forms of help are possible.

As a result, your request for information may be a veil for the actual information you need, or for some other kind of obstacle. (See "Finding the Key Obstacle," page 177.)

Before giving you the information that you ask for, I will do best if I determine why you need the information and what you already know. Then I can tailor my presentation to be most helpful to you.

If I do not determine your situation first, I risk giving you information that hinders or distracts you from attaining your goals.

✧ THE THREE GUIDES ✧

Once, a wise princess arrived at an inn on the road to Baghdad. When she told the occupants that she sought a guide for her journey, three applicants presented themselves.

The princess said, "I will hire the one of you who best assists the next traveler entering this inn."

Soon, a traveler arrived. After a brief conversation with the first guide, the traveler picked up his bags to continue his journey.

Before the traveler could leave the inn, however, the second guide approached him. In a few moments, the traveller put down his bags to stay the night.

Immediately, the third guide began conversing with the traveler. Resolutely, the traveler picked up his bags and returned the way he had come.

The wise princess asked the guides how they had helped the traveler.

The first guide said, "He asked me the way to

Baghdad. I gave him concise, clear directions. But I fear the progress of his journey has been halted and then reversed by the ineptitude of the other two guides."

The second guide said, "I was not inept. I asked him why he traveled to Baghdad. He told me that he sought a store where he could buy a megaphone. 'You are in luck!' I said. 'Such a store exists in this very village, and will be open in the morning.' But I fear the third guide, in his gruffness, has discouraged the traveler from staying the night."

"Ah!" said the third guide. "I was not gruff. I merely asked him why he wanted a megaphone in the first place. He said, 'I have learned that a megaphone will allow me to sing the holy hymns to hundreds at a time!' "

The third guide continued, "I asked him further, 'How many normally listen when you sing without a megaphone?' Seeing his perplexed expression, I enlightened him. 'It is true, traveler, that a megaphone will do what you wish—but only if you already know how to sing the holy hymns.' The traveler is now returning to his own village to study with a teacher of singing."

The wise princess hired the third guide.

When the Information May Already Have Been Received

Part of my role is to notice whether you've received the information.

This means not stopping before you have understood.

This also means stopping as soon as you have understood.

I must keep my focus on you and your needs, even as I explore the knowledge that you need. I must pay attention to what you are showing me and telling me.

Even as I share my knowledge with you, I must remain your servant.

Coaching to Overcome The Second Obstacle: Needing More Experience of the Story

Many times, the obstacle to your success is lack of information.

Many more times, the obstacle is of another kind.

The most common obstacles are that you need to imagine the story more, or that you need to determine more clearly what the story means to you.

In general terms, these obstacles involve the need to imagine the details and meaning of your project or presentation. I call these obstacles "needing more experience of the story."

The Essence of Guy's Story

In a coaching workshop, Guy told a story about two brothers. The narrator and his younger brother, Benjie, were befriended by a policeman, Mr. Moon, after Mr. Moon apprehended Benjie stealing. Here's an excerpt:

"Now, Mr. Moon came and started taking Benjie and me out to baseball games. He started telling us stories. He started coming over in the evenings and helping us do our homework. He started taking care of us.

"One day, Benjie and me and Mr. Moon and all of our sisters went on a picnic in his big old Volkswagen car. After that time, Benjie became a changed person."

Guy's story was beautiful: understated, moving, and delicate.

With Guy's permission, I had the workshop members give appreciations. He told us during the appreciations that his story was inspired by an actual incident in which he had caught a child stealing—and the child had begun to cry, saying, "Nobody loves me enough." Guy had tried to help the boy, but felt unsuccessful. As a result, he created a story in which Mr. Moon succeeded in changing Benjie through loving attention.

When Guy agreed to hear suggestions, I began with a question:

Coach: *Is there a place or a part of it where you'd like help?*

Guy: *When I usually tell it to young people I tell them the real story behind it, of the real confrontation I had with that boy, to show them how I can model something different in a life.*

Coach: *So, your motivation for the story is really the role of Mr. Moon?*

Guy: *Showing it through the story. I find that storytelling allows me to bring that "touching" to them without being invasive.*

As coach, I had no initial basis for helping Guy improve his story. But once he told me that his goal was to show how Mr. Moon had been helpful, I could compare what he had achieved with what he wanted to achieve. Now I could judge for myself: was the story showing how Mr. Moon interacted with Benjie?

My answer was, "Not yet." Guy had only summarized the crucial parts of the interaction with sentences like, "[we all] went on a picnic ...." I was not left with a strong sense of how Mr. Moon had caused the change in Benjie.

So far, I had determined that Guy had a goal which he was not achieving as well as he might. Therefore, I knew there had to be some obstacle.

BEYOND NEEDING INFORMATION

What is Guy's obstacle? Guy might need information—if some lack of information is preventing him from showing us the interaction between Benjie and Mr. Moon. It's much more likely, however, that his obstacle is needing to imagine the story more fully at this crucial point.

I told Guy that we needed more details that would allow us to imagine the interaction. Once he understood what I meant, he was very receptive:

Coach: *To me, the only thing that would make Mr. Moon even more powerful would be a few details that we could imagine.*

Guy: *About him?*

Coach: *About him or the interaction—because the interaction's what you really love.*

Guy: *OK. Because I just told you the story about the interaction, but I didn't create the interaction.*

Coach: *Exactly. And so it's just picking up the details. The picnic—even one detail about what happened, one picture of Mr. Moon, how he was, or how Benjie was before or after interacting. Just one little picture of him. You don't have to tell us about it, you can show us the whole picture.*

Guy: *I can see it. I'm starting to see it.*

Coach: *Great! You want to share any of what you see?*

Guy: *Yeah. After that, Mr. Moon started coming over, and he used to help us with our homework, and he used to take us to baseball games.*

And Benjie, he used to dive-bomb—to run himself up on his back.

Coach: *Yeah, that's the stuff. You see how that does it. Is that an OK place to stop?*

Already, the image of Benjie "dive-bombing" Mr. Moon is beginning to add texture to this important section of the story. Clearly, Guy knows how to overcome this obstacle, now that his attention has been directed toward it. Since Guy can continue easily without me, my job is done for now.

If I had time in Guy's coaching session, of course, it might make sense for me to listen to more of Guy's imaginings—while they are flowing so well. But it would not make sense for me to make up details for him. Guy can create them for himself.

A crucial step was to discover Guy's main goal for his story. There are many places in his story where he could add additional details, but adding them to the core of the story will intensify—rather than dilute—the story's forcefulness.

Imagining a Crucial Scene

From Guy's session, we see how gaining more experience of your story (or presentation) can mean imagining your story more—especially in the parts that add to your central meaning.

Sometimes, this imagining leads to adding new details to a scene, as in Guy's story. Other times, it leads to creating a whole new scene. Still other times, it leads to a new way of performing the same scene.

Creating a New Scene

Betty told a folktale to a coaching workshop. The hero of her story is the leader of a band of pilgrims crossing a desert. In the midst of their journey the pilgrims are surrounded by brigands, and the hero meets the leader of the brigands atop a dune. Since they speak no common language, they converse in impromptu signs. At the end of their "conversation," the brigands hurry off in fear, and the pilgrims continue in safety. As in all such folktales, the two leaders interpret the signs differently. The story ends with the holy hero describing the supposed holiness of the brigand chief, and the fierce leader of the brigands describing the supposed fierceness of the pilgrims.

After we listened and gave appreciations, I asked Betty if she wanted to hear suggestions. One workshop participant noted that Betty seemed to lose energy as she spoke the very last lines:

"And that is how the pilgrims arrived safely on another's day segment of their journey to the Holy Land, while the marauding band ran as fast as they could—scattering dust and their gold booty on the sands—to get away from this terrible, fearsome tribe."

Betty responded in a way that suggested her obstacle: "Part of the problem is that the ending that I've heard, I don't like. The ending that I've heard is, 'That's the first time in history that a lack of communication worked out well on both sides.' And to me, that's not the heart of the story. The heart of the story is the purity of this guy, who in the face of danger didn't even see it. I was making up my own ending, poorly."

Betty clearly knew her goals for the story, its "heart." Her obstacle was in applying those goals to the final scene.

With her permission, I began to help her create a more consistent ending. First, we needed a more specific statement of her understanding of the story:

Coach: *Keep talking about the meaning.*

Betty: *The purity of his heart, the goodness of his heart wouldn't allow him to see danger, even when there was danger. And likewise, the robbers saw evil where there wasn't evil.*

I noticed that she mentioned the contrasting attitude of the brigand, as well. This brought up a choice: should her ending image contain both of their attitudes, or just one?

Coach: *Do you think the end needs to speak to both of those?*

Betty: *I don't want it to be a moral. That's what I'm trying to avoid.*

Coach: *We can do what you want by using parting images, rather than a statement of what they were like.*

Betty: *OK.*

Coach: *But do you want them both, or just one?*

Betty: *I guess I'd rather stick with just the pilgrims.*

At this point, Betty had agreed to seek an image—not a statement—that exemplified the hero's attitude of seeing goodness even where there is evil. My job was to help Betty create such an image:

Coach: *How do you see this pure man leaving the confab on the dune? What's your parting glimpse of him?*

Betty: *I see him casually and gratefully walking away. You know, like how lucky it was to get blessed with an extra treat on this trip. And he's packing up casually.*

This attempt did not quite work. Betty needed an image that contained more of the qualities that she wanted to show in her hero.

Coach: *We're looking for a simple brush stroke that suggests the whole image. We want the qualities you mentioned: his gratitude, his calmness, and his blithe ignorance of the danger. Right?*

Betty: *Yes.*

Coach: *Is there a gesture he'd make? A little action he would take?*

Betty: *Could he offer a prayer of thanksgiving or something like that?*

Coach: *Try it.*

Betty: *While on the other side of the mountain, the leader of the pilgrims called them all together, and they offered a prayer of thanksgiving, especially for this encounter. And then they went on to the Holy Land.*

Betty was getting closer. Now she had an action that incorporated her hero's attitude, but only in a general way. She needed to get more specific. I reminded her of how she had been specific in the earlier parts of her story:

Coach: *All through this story, we saw him. He was such a great character. So let our parting shot of him be like a documentary movie, where we see him doing something with his beads around his neck or the stuff on his camel or his holy prayer book. Let us really picture him there. Do you see what I mean?*

Betty: *Yes.*

Coach: *What would his attitude be toward the departing brigands?*

Betty: *Maybe he'd offer them a blessing on their journey?*

Coach: *Imagine that in detail, then tell us what you see.*

Betty: *Yes. [long pause] Slowly, reverently, he mounted his camel. He looked longingly at the dust of the fleeing brigands. Then he burst out in prayer. "May you have a safe journey, my newfound friends! And may we learn goodness from you, who are so eager to proceed to your next act of holiness!"*

Now Betty had succeeded. All along, she had known what the story meant to her, and that she had not wanted to end the story with a "moral." But she needed my help to imagine a scene that embodied the qualities she saw in her hero. My job consisted largely of holding out to her the possibility that she could create such a scene, and insisting that she imagine it in great detail.

It does not matter, by the way, whether Betty will use this exact image in future tellings of this story. It matters only that she now knows how to create an image that serves her vision of what the story means.

PERFORMING A SCENE WITH HEART

In a coaching workshop, Amy told a spiritual story from India about a generous king who wishes to know what else he should be giving his subjects. In response, a dove enters his palace, fleeing from a hawk. When the dove asks for safety, the king pledges protection. But the hawk enters and demands the dove, which is his food.

The king asks the hawk what substitute it will accept; the hawk agrees to take an equal amount of flesh from any creature. Now the king realizes that he can not in justice kill any creature in his kingdom. He offers, then, an equal amount of his own flesh.

The king erects a scale with the dove in one pan. He cuts a piece of his own thigh and puts it on the other pan; the scale does not tilt. He cuts larger and larger pieces, to the same effect.

Finally, the king understands that he must offer himself completely. He throws himself onto the scale. At that moment, the scale disappears, the king is made whole, and a god appears. The god congratulates the king for finally understanding what he should offer his subjects, and offers him a place in Paradise.

During the appreciation period, workshop members mentioned the emotional intensity of Amy's performance. Yet I felt unconvinced in some way. Some piece of the emotional transformation of the king was missing for me.

During the suggestion period, I asked Amy what the story was about for her. She replied, "He's been giving. And he desires to give. But he's not sure that he has ever given enough. And I also think there's a faith piece. Like maybe before he cuts into his thigh, he says, 'And yet, what will happen when this is gone and when I am gone?' "

After I asked more questions, I learned that the key moment for Amy is when the king, seeing that his half-measures are not working, decides to throw his entire body into the balance pan. At this moment, he stops measuring his offerings, and decides to offer everything. Suddenly, the question "Have I given enough?" is no longer relevant: he has given everything, enough or not.

This scene, I also realized, was the scene that failed to convince me as a listener. Now that Amy had explored more consciously the meaning of this scene for her, however, it seemed that she might perform it more convincingly. I asked Amy to try telling the scene again.

The result was not much improved.

At this point, either I had not completely identified the obstacle, or I had not yet found out how to help her overcome it. Since I suspected that I had identified the correct obstacle, the question was, how could I help her overcome it?

I tried giving Amy a chance to listen—to imagine without having to speak—while I summarized for her this part of her story. I said:

"Think of how the king approaches the world before he throws himself on the scale. He means well, but he is measuring his gifts. Now think of how he approaches the world after that moment of decision. He gives everything and doesn't worry about measuring. Can you imagine the change?"

Amy replied, "He has entered into the path of grace."

On an impulse, I added, "Can you find that path of grace in your body? Can you feel it physically?" After a moment, Amy said she could. I said, "Now find the frenzy of measuring that comes right before that. Can you find that in your body, too?"

When Amy replied that she could, I asked her to tell the scene again. "And this time, feel those two states. Take your time when he changes from measuring into grace. Don't throw yourself on the balance until you fully feel the 'path of grace.' "

This time, her performance had an emotional depth that left us breathless.

Amy had needed help experiencing her story more fully. The crucial scene could only take its place in the story if she understood its relationship to what the story meant to her. Further, she could only perform this scene convincingly if she could imagine the internal transformation of the king as she described it. For her, finding the physical sensations associated with the "before" and "after" emotional states of the king allowed her to experience the story more fully. This, in turn, allowed us, her listeners, to experience the transformation for ourselves.

Note that Betty (in the previous section) did well to imagine the scene visually, whereas Amy did better when I focused her attention on bodily sensations. My role as coach included finding what the story meant to Amy, as usual. At the same time, it included finding a sensory mode that would allow Amy to imagine the emotions as well as the events.

Imagining the Story Structure

When I help you gain more experience of the story, I may help you with a single scene—to add to it, create it, or perform it.

I may also help you with the story as a whole. Your obstacle may relate to a sequence of scenes, a string of moments throughout your story, or with the decision of what to include in the story.

A SEQUENCE OF SCENES

Ned told his own version of the traditional Chinese tale "The Stonecutter." In it, Jack starts as a humble stonecutter, then wishes to be a prince and is magically transformed into one. As the prince, Jack realizes that he is less powerful than the sun, and wishes to become the sun. In turn, Jack becomes the cloud that blocks the sun, the wind that blows the cloud, and the mountain that stops the wind. Finally, he wishes to become the humble stonecutter, who alone is more powerful than the mountain.

Ned's telling of this story had many clever twists of thought and delightful Appalachian localisms. Yet it seemed lacking in overall shape. Perhaps Ned's obstacle was needing more experience of the story's structure.

I asked Ned what he loved about the story. This dialogue resulted:

Coach: *Now that you just told it, what do you like about the story?*

Ned: *It tells us that we can be happy within ourselves. We don't have to be anyone else. We're responsible for our own happiness. And things aren't always as good as they look.*

Coach: *Tell me how that comes out in the story.*

Ned: *The stonecutter is happy with his work. He's perfectly satisfied with his whole life—until he sees something better.*

Coach: *He's satisfied? So, the first time, it takes a lot to make him dissatisfied. Is that right?*

Ned: *Yes. He asks to be turned into a prince, but he gets more demanding each time. He's really getting less satisfied, but he doesn't know it until the end.*

What I heard Ned saying was that the progression goes from "satisfied" to "highly dissatisfied" back to "very satisfied" when Jack finally becomes a stonecutter again. The emotional milestones along the way are his increasingly demanding requests to be transformed into the next character.

It seemed, then, that if Ned could make the series of demands have a clear emotional shape, then the story as a whole might have a clear emotional shape. The series might be written like this:

The stonecutter wishes to be the prince [satisfied].
The prince wishes to be the sun [slightly dissatisfied].
The sun wishes to be the wind [moderately dissatisfied].
The wind wishes to be the cloud [very dissatisfied].

The cloud wishes to be the mountain [highly dissatisfied].
The mountain wishes to be the stonecutter [hugely dissatisfied].
The stonecutter resumes his work [very satisfied].

The first and last emotional states are satisfied. In between are five degrees of dissatisfaction.

To express five distinct degrees of any emotion can be challenging. One way to approach this challenge is to first establish the extremes, then to fill in the three intermediate stages. I asked Ned to try the most dissatisfied demand, when the mountain wishes to be the stonecutter.

His first attempt at sounding dissatisfied came out quite tame. Clearly, he could not build up to this low level in five stages; he sounded like he was on the first stage, at most.

Therefore, Ned needed help expressing this feeling. I began with a question:

Coach: *How does Jack (as the mountain) feel when he realizes that there is someone hacking him to bits?*

Ned: *He feels anger, because he wants to be the most powerful thing and he isn't.*

Coach: *He had changed and changed again, always to be the most powerful thing, and now, once again, he sees something still more powerful. Is that right?*

Ned: *Yes.*

Coach: *Can you let me hear what that would sound like?*

In response, Ned made a sound that convinced us that he was angry and dissatisfied. I said:

Coach: *Where did you feel that in your body?*

Ned: *In my throat. No, more in my gut.*

Coach: *Great! So you can feel some anger in your throat, but the big source of it is in your gut. Is that right?*

Ned: *Yes, I'd say so.*

Coach: *That gives you a new possibility. Try feeling a smaller anger that's just in your throat. Let's say when Jack wants to be the wind.*

Ned's "throat anger" was less demanding than this "gut

anger," but it was still recognizably demanding.

Coach: *One way to keep track of a sequence of feelings is to string them out along a single dimension. The obvious one here is up and down along your torso. Do you want to try it?*

With Ned's consent, I helped him choose five physical locations in which he could feel his anger: the crown of his head, his nose, his throat, his chest, and his gut. When he imagined his dissatisfaction coming from each of these points in turn, he produced five increasing shades of anger. They were not always strictly distinguishable to his audience, but Ned's awareness of his "location" along his torso worked to keep him aware of how far he had come in the emotional progression and how far he had yet to go.

Along the way, I had given Ned information about using a body dimension to keep track of a sequence of feelings. This technique is not appropriate for every teller or every story, of course, but it worked for Ned in this case. If he had responded differently to my question about where he felt the anger in his body, I would have approached his problem differently. For example, if he had said, "I don't feel it in my body. I just imagine somebody who hurt me and made me angry," then I would have tried to find five degrees of anger based on people who hurt him. He might have been able to imagine five different offenses, or people of five different sizes, or people with five different weapons.

My role in this session, once I had elicited Ned's goals for the story, was to help Ned give an overall emotional shape to his performance. Once he had the information about using a single physical dimension, I was able to help him "measure" the progress of the story along his own body. Thus, he gained new experience of the shape of his story.

RESTRUCTURING THE STORY

Derek came to a coaching workshop with a story from his childhood. In the story, young Derek decides to hatch a chicken's egg. At the end of the story, in the heat of a clapping game, he forgets about the egg in his pocket. The story ends this way:

Well, when I hit that egg, I felt something kind of wet and slimy roll down my leg. And I looked down, and there was yellow yolk on my feet. I found out that I hadn't picked the egg for hatching; I had picked the egg for eating. That's a true story.

One of the suggestions that other workshop members made about Derek's story was to improve the last line, "That's a true story." I asked Derek if he wanted my help to work on the ending.

At this point, I didn't know what the obstacle was. So I asked Derek a question—to see how much he had already experienced the story.

Coach: *So, what changed in your life as a result of this incident?*

Derek: *Well, my desire to hatch chickens changed.*

Coach: *Uh-huh. Tell me more. Keep talking.*

Derek: *[Pauses.] I think probably as I think about it now as an adult, I learned to respect some aspect of nature, that as a human being I don't have as much control over it. That there are some things that are much more fragile than others, that should be left to nature.*

This was the central meaning of the story for Derek—and he wasn't aware of it until I asked him the question.

At this point, I was able to build a vague conception of the finished story, around the central theme. Without knowing any specifics, I knew that when the story finds its mature form, each scene will be part of the unfolding of the central meaning that Derek had just articulated. The ending will be the view of the central meaning that Derek wants to leave us with.

Derek's task now was to apply what he had just learned about the meaning of his story to every scene in it—including some scenes from his childhood that he may not yet have linked to this story at all.

To help Derek tackle this task, I listed the major scenes in the story as he had told it—so he could think about which ones actually related to the meaning he wanted. After summarizing the story as he told it, I asked him:

Coach: *Did any of those parts feel like, "Oh, this is about intervening in nature versus letting it alone."*

Derek: *As you were talking I started to think about something, and that is that my grandmother also had, apart from chickens, pigs. I saw pigs with little piglets, I saw chickens with little chicklets. And so here were little families. And the thing about going to my grandmother's house was that here's a part of my family. This is very much a family experience.*

I continued to interview Derek about this theme from his childhood. Derek remembered another scene from his childhood, and talked about how each scene related to his central meaning—namely, learning about the fragility of nature, and our limitations as humans when we try to interfere with nature.

After a while, I brought Derek's attention back to the ending.

Coach: *Good! So there are two new parts to this story that fit into this theme, that weren't in the story before. And one is Grandma taking care of you, and you being in some ways her chicken, her chick, and you wanting to have a chick to play with.*

Derek: *Right.*

Coach: *So those might belong in the story, to make that theme. If that's the way it goes, if those are the strong emotional parts of the setup, then how is the end? Emotionally, what's in the ending, then?*

Derek: *I think the fact that I find out that I can't create this particular family by myself allows me to appreciate what is there.*

Now, for the first time, Derek will be able to discover a fitting ending to the story—because he has explored the story, experiencing how it related to larger themes than he had previously guessed.

Derek: *I always thought of this as a little throwaway story. I never thought, "How did this act have an effect on my life later on?" And of course now, as I'm thinking about it, I'm suddenly realizing there's something about this story that has stayed in my memory for this long, and two, probably therefore had quite a powerful impact on how I think about the world and how I think about things.*

Coach: *Is there anything else you'd like?*

Derek: *Just some time to process it and retell it.*

Derek still needed time to live with the new images he discovered before he would be able to decide exactly where each one would go.

Then, in his own time, he would be able to choose an ending image or scene that shows what he wanted to show: a boy disappointed in his failure to change nature by creating his own little family of chicks, but at the same time much more appreciative of the family that he does have.

My role was to help Derek realize what the story was about for him, and then to help him reconstruct the story so that it would convey the meaning he chose. He needed to be interviewed about the events in his past that might relate to his theme, then encouraged to choose those that let his theme be introduced, intensified, and finally resolved.

Experiencing the Narrator

When you tell a personal experience story, you may have special problems not usually faced by tellers of traditional tales. The personal story comes to you without a clear narrative shape, often without a predetermined beginning or end. More subtly, the most important character may be hidden behind the "I" of your narrator. To discover and develop that character requires thorough experience of the story.

As your coach, if I know this common problem for tellers of personal stories, I can be alert for it. Yet if I say to you, "Put yourself in the story," you will probably not know what to do. I may need to lead you step-by-step through some of the process, then sketch out for you how to complete it.

WINONA'S STORY

Winona told a true-life humorous story about her absent-minded former husband. She described Will as the "kind of man who gets so caught up in his own thoughts that he just stops—usually, in a doorway." She described how he frequently left his dirty socks on the living room floor. One day, disgusted at picking up his laundry, she left his favorite pair of navy-blue knee socks where he had left them, in the center of the living room. She left them there for three months. Finally, on the day of a party at their house, she asked him somewhat peevishly to move them. Apologetic, he said, "Winona, all you have to do is ask!" Then he lifted up the cushion on the couch, put the socks under it, and replaced the cushion. As far as Winona knows, the socks are still there!

Clearly, this was an entertaining anecdote. To gain an additional layer of depth, however, Winona may need to experience the story more fully. In particular, she might examine her role as the character who narrates. I got my first hints of what she had left out of the story when she responded to my appreciation:

Coach: *I really loved it when, after three months, you said to him, "I don't want to nag."*

Winona: *Every word in that story is true. In fact, it went on. It got to be an elaborate game. Everybody but Will knew about the socks. Other people would occasionally come in and make some excuse to move the socks.*

When I continued my appreciation of the same line from the story, Winona gave a further statement of her attitude toward the events of the story:

Coach: *It's a great line, because it's such an understatement by now.*

Winona: *Actually, after a while it became a game, and I thoroughly enjoyed it.*

Since this was still the time for appreciations, I did not respond further, but took note of what she had revealed.

ESTABLISHING THE MAIN THEME

When it came time for suggestions, I asked about her goals,

in the form of asking about her connection to the story:

Coach: *What do you love about the story?*

Winona: *If I had to find a moral in it, apart from it's just funny, I'd say ....*

I interrupted her immediately, because it was clear she misunderstood my question. She confused "meaning" with seriousness, or with giving the story a self-conscious moral. But following her love of the humor led to finding the shape of the story:

Coach: *Funny is funny! You don't have to go anywhere else to find what you love. What's funny about it?*

Winona: *It's just ridiculous that two grown people could leave a pair of socks in the middle of the floor for three months! He wasn't aware of it. That was ridiculous. My part was a way to cope with things that you know are going to make a great story later on, but they're not a lot of fun right now.*

Coach: *So, in fact—not in the story you told, but in your life experience—it was a frustrating situation.*

Winona: *It started out that way. There were a lot of other things that I just dealt with. Like, "I have no idea why you left a cup in the bathtub, but I'll pick it up. But I won't pick up those damn socks!"*

Coach: *So if you decide to put more of yourself in the story, that sounds like the place to look: at your coping mechanism for sharing space with this difficult person.*

At this point, we had identified the theme of her narrator's journey in the story—namely, how she coped with her husband's frustrating absentmindedness. Now, we could go on to explore that theme:

Coach: *I suggest brainstorming all the things that have to do with your reaction to his absent-mindedness—and with your changing reaction: your frustration, for example. The cup in the bathtub is funny! Do you remember the first time you realized that this guy was absent-minded?*

Winona: *I'd seen symptoms all along, but I guess they just didn't sink in. Because he could never remember what he had done with anything. He was one of these people who will stand in the middle of a room and say, "Somebody's stolen my socks!"*

Coach: *That's good! Did you realize this about him before or after you got married to him?*

Winona: *I guess I realized it before, but while dating one tends to find things somewhat more amusing.*

Coach: *Good! That leaves the possibility of starting back with the amusement.*

Winona: *Yeah.*

Coach: *And moving to frustration and then to the amusement of the "game."*

Winona: *Sure.*

Winona's tone conveyed her excitement about taking the story in this direction. Assured that we were pursuing goals that she was willing to adopt (at least for now), I turned my attention to helping her find a moment of transition between amusement and frustration.

Coach: *Do you remember that first moment of frustration?*

Winona: *I can't remember exactly, but it was something to do with the refrigerator, and I think it was he put the wrong thing in the refrigerator. And left what would spoil out. It was! It was a gallon of milk. And he put something else in the refrigerator, and left the milk out. We were poor as church mice, and he let a gallon of milk go bad that we could hardly afford in the first place. And I think that was when I stopped laughing.*

Note that Winona thought at first that she could not remember this incident. Once she began to tell about it, however, she remembered a great deal of it.

GIVING THE STORY A SHAPE

By now, we had found the two early stages of Winona's coping—amusement, then frustration—as well as the turning point between them, which was the incident of the spoiled milk. We already knew that the "knee socks" development was the final stage of "amusement." I drew her a simple diagram of her story's hypothetical new shape.

figure 1: The Hypothetical Shape of Winona's Story

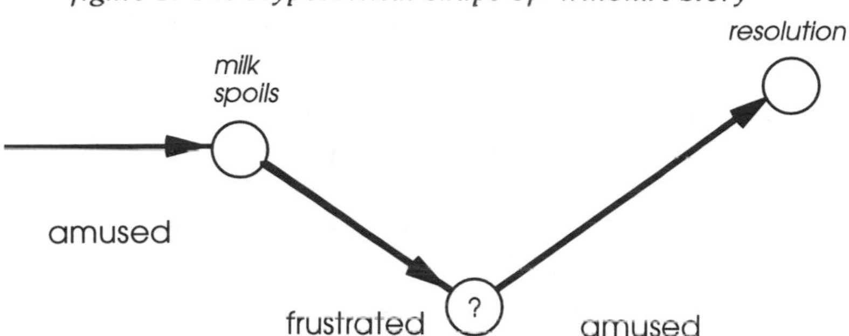

Coach: *[draws diagram as speaks] So, if you go with this outline of amusing-frustrating-amusing, then it's like this.*

Here on the left is your early time with this dear man with the quirky qualities, which are amusing in their own way [traces finger along the first "amused" segment].

And then the moment happens when the gallon of milk gets left out to spoil, and we start to see a different movement, which goes all the way to some culminating moment [points to circle with question mark]—I'm not sure what it is yet, we're looking for this one—when you decide you're going to make it a game again. And then we have the whole thing with the socks [points to the second "amused" segment].

And then we need some kind of resolution. It might be too soon to know what it is until you've mapped out more of the rest of it. But then, having generated a nice long list of these incidents, you will choose the ones that seem to work best to make these "builds" happen.

Next, I explained more of the process that would happen on other days, after she had fished for new incidents and made a new draft of her story:

Coach: *Then you tell the whole thing and after telling it you realize, "Oh, actually it has to go a little further and add something else on the end." Or you realize, "That's great, but I didn't need so much in the first segment, I can cut that out or combine three incidents into one." That's the process. Does that give you enough to go on?*

Winona: *Yeah, I think so. I had been thinking of it as events that happened, rather than my reaction.*

Coach: *Yes! What we've added here is your reaction.*

My role was first to notice that the "journey" of Winona's narrator had not yet been included in the story. Then, working from what she loved about the story, I elicited from her the narrator's emotional story. My questions focused on the main stages of her reaction and on the moments of transition.

Next, I gave her a diagram to express my hypothesis of the story's shape, and checked it with her. Then I explained the parts of the process that remained for her to do. Since Winona agreed with my hypothesis and seemed clear at this point about what to do, my job was done for today.

Of course, Winona is free to change her mind about any part of this. She may come to a new understanding of what she loves about the story or of what the story should include. If my hypothesis proves incorrect, though, it will not mean that our time together was wasted. On the contrary, my hypothesis—as long as I clearly identify it as only a starting point—will have served to focus her efforts and to give her something against which she can profitably react.

Questions: The Tool of Choice

When you lack information (as discussed in the previous chapter), you need something external to your presentation. You need answers.

When you need more experience of your story, however, you need to explore your inner world. You need to be guided through your own stories, your own values, your own imagination. You need questions—and a non-judgmental listener to the answers you find within.

Questions, in fact, are my most important tool for helping you with the obstacle of needing more experience of your story.

A PALETTE OF QUESTIONS

Just as a painter needs a supply of brushes with varied shapes and degree of stiffness, as your coach I need a palette of questions for various purposes and situations.

A more accurate comparison might be with the painter's oil colors. The painter keeps a supply of stock colors on hand, but is skilled in mixing them to create a unique color for each painted shape. Similarly, I use different basic forms of questions to create unique tools for each coaching session.

As described in "Asking Questions" (page 72), I blend closed-ended questions with open-ended questions, depending on my desire to focus on a particular piece of information or to invite you to explore a wider area.

The closed-ended questions let me clarify specific points, or to translate something from one form of expression to another, or to summarize and verify what you said:

Coach: *Do you think the end needs to speak of those?*

Coach: *Can you let me hear what that would sound like?*

Coach: *He's satisfied? So, the first time, it takes a lot to make him dissatisfied. Is that right?*

The bulk of my questions in this chapter are open-ended questions, since my goal is to have you explore some aspect of your own experience. Of these, the most important questions are the ones that ask your primary goal, intention, or connection to the story you are telling (or the proposal you are processing, or the future factory you are imagining):

Coach: *What do you love about the story?*

Coach: *So, what changed in your life as a result of this incident?*

Coach: *What's funny about your story?*

Other open-ended questions are simply requests to keep talking, to expand on what you've said:

Coach: *Then what happened?*

Coach: *How do you see this pure man leaving the confab on the dune? What's your parting glimpse of him?*

BRINGING IT BACK TO YOUR STORY

When I help you experience a story more fully, I am an active listener to your story. Although the story remains yours, I take part in eliciting it.

Each such coaching session itself resembles a story: the story of how you learned about your story.

My role in this "story" is to ask questions that guide your attention in various directions. First, I may direct you to look at the meaning of the story, or of some incident in it. Then I may help you face away from the story to other incidents in your life or the life of your characters. Next, I may suggest that you try to perform what you have just described.

After you've mentioned and described something that seems related to your goals for your story, for example, I can use a question to bring out how it relates to the physical action of the story (e.g., "How does Jack, as the mountain, feel when he realizes that there is someone hacking him to bits?").

A question can also help you search for a turning point (e.g., "Do you remember the first time you got it that this guy was absent-minded?").

Similarly, a question can help you select images of memories that serve a particular function in your story (e.g., "Did any of those parts feel like, 'Oh, this is about intervening in nature versus letting it alone.' ").

GUIDED-FANTASY QUESTIONS

None of the sessions described in this chapter required the use of guided-fantasy questions, which are questions about freely generated images that may or may not ever become part of your story. Such questions can be vital to helping certain storytellers.

Let's look back at Derek's and Winona's sessions. When asked for the main points of their stories, they gave straightforward statements. Each of them gave a misleading first reply, but came soon to a statement of the essence of each story. Derek said, "I learned to respect some aspect of nature ...," and

Winona said, "a way to cope with things that are ... not a lot of fun right now."

Not all tellers come so quickly to such rationalistic descriptions. Some tellers need to work in the world of images or of physical sensations while they are expanding their experience of the story.

Jay was such a teller. He came to me with an original story he wanted to publish on audiocassette. When he told it, I did not think it was ready for recording.

I began the suggestion period by asking a form of the fundamental question about goals:

Coach: *What draws you to this story?*

Jay: *I haven't thought of that for a while. I guess it's the sparkle in Jeremy's eyes.*

Coach: *Tell me about the sparkle.*

At this point, Jay might have responded in the language of exposition, saying something like, "Well, it seems that he has this indomitable spirit ...." If so, it would have made sense to continue as I had with Derek or Winona.

In fact, Jay responded by describing images:

Jay: *I keep thinking of the incident with his uncle when Jeremy was three years old. His aunt knew that nothing could dim the sparkle in Jeremy's eyes .... And then, when Jeremy is older and falls in love, ...*

From this, I understood that Jay's internal knowledge of what belonged in this story was tied to images, not to concepts.

Therefore, my questions needed to elicit images.

First, we needed to collect the "sparkle" images already present in the story. I said:

Coach: *Are you willing to explore this theme of Jeremy's sparkle a little?*

Jay: *Sure. It is what calls to me in the story.*

Coach: *Where else does it come out in the story?*

After Jay had described a miscellany of story incidents—some of them well developed, others just fragments—I tried using a guided fantasy question to elicit more images of Jeremy's central struggle:

Coach: *Imagine Jeremy lying in bed at night. He is sleepless, because he has some vague sense of the purpose of his life, but no idea what to actually do. The moonlight casts the moving shadow of a tree on his bedroom wall. Suddenly, Jeremy recognizes a shape in the shadow. What shape is it?*

"Guided imagery" questions like this one are similar to inkblots. They give Jay an opportunity to project his still unconscious knowledge about Jeremy onto interesting but indefinite situations.

These questions often need to come in groups. I asked Jay about four or five such questions before his own sense of Jeremy's "sparkle" took over, and he began creating images without my help. Here's another example, based on answers Jay had given to earlier questions—answers that sent Jeremy to the city to gain wealth:

Coach: *Jeremy has been in the city, far from home, for several years. One day, he is walking along the city street thinking of his job and how he wants to get rich. Suddenly, his eyes light on something in a store window that reminds him of some part of home that he deeply misses. What does he see? What does he miss?*

Few or none of Jay's answers became part of the final story. But they helped elicit the essence of the story, which was the rise, fall, and re-emergence of Jeremy's sparkle. This process prompted Jay to re-open his imaginative investigation of a story that he had thought was already finished—without me needing to say, "The story isn't ready."

In this session, Jay found it relatively easy to answer my guided-fantasy questions. His answers led him on to a greater understanding of Jeremy's sparkle and how it would work itself out in a plot. Another storyteller, however, might have found these questions threatening or useless—as Jay himself might have, at another time or with another story. If the questions didn't help, of course, I would drop this kind of question after one or two tries. Usually, if this kind of question is inappropriate, the presenter will start spontaneously on another kind of thinking. I need only pay attention, remain flexible, and follow the presenter's lead.

Coaching to Overcome The Third Obstacle: Misdirected Effort

If you lack information, I give it to you.

If you lack experience of your story (or other presentation or project), I try to lead you to imagine it and its meanings more fully.

But sometimes your obstacle is not a lack, but a surplus. You may be making efforts that detract from your presentation.

In this case, you are misdirecting some of your effort.

For the coach, this is the most delicate obstacle. Because you are making things worse by trying the wrong thing, I am in danger of adding more wrong things for you to try.

My Evil Landowner

Here's an example from my own storytelling.

In a story about an evil landowner who is exploiting peasants, I portrayed the landowner with bombast—dramatically, loudly and harshly. Although the bombast was obvious to any perceptive listener, the story as a whole was well received, in spite of my own sense that something wasn't quite right.

What was my obstacle?

Might it have been lack of information? Maybe I just didn't know that the bombast was repelling people? This is possible, but there would have to be another obstacle preventing me from noticing that they were repelled—and this might be the main obstacle.

Might my obstacle have been needing more experience of the story? Maybe I didn't know what the evil landowner meant to me, or his role in the story?

This was not the case. If a coach had asked me what the evil landowner meant I could have answered clearly and accurately.

As it turned out, I was trying to do something that didn't need to be done. I was misdirecting some of my effort. The ineffective bombast was merely a symptom of an unconscious misconception.

I had assumed incorrectly that evil had to be something external to me—that the audience and I both had to hold ourselves apart from the evil landowner. In other words, my bombast was distancing me from the character—intentionally.

Until I corrected this misconception, nothing told me by a coach could have really helped. Suppose a coach said, "Do that character more quietly." How would I have responded? Still imagining that my job was to separate myself from the character's evil, I would have found a quiet way to do that same job. The result might not have been bombast, but it wouldn't have been effective storytelling, either. The connection to myself—and the audience—would still have been missing.

But my coach noticed what I was doing, and found a way to help me notice it. He asked, "Is there a part of you that is like that landowner?"

My first response was to think, "No, of course not." But the moment I was conscious of my own thought, I realized that it was incorrect. In a flash, I understood what I had been doing.

As soon as I found the part of myself that is just as evil as that landowner, I could play the scenes quietly. Finally, I could redirect my effort into connecting with the character, instead of misdirecting my effort toward disconnection.

A coach who did not help me go through this process would not have been helpful—in spite of being correct about the symptoms of my obstacle.

THE KINDS OF MISDIRECTED EFFORT

Sometimes you (like me in the previous example) may have a misconception about performance technique. Other times you may misdirect effort toward gaining the audience's approval or interest. Still other times you may put effort into something that protects you from an unpleasant feeling about your audience or your story—but at the cost of decreased effectiveness.

As coach, I need to notice each kind of effort, help you notice it, then help you redirect your effort more profitably.

Misconceptions About Performance

In a coaching workshop, Brenda stood up with a piece of paper in her hands, saying she couldn't actually tell her story yet but had to read it. She read it well. But her reading lacked the relaxation, immediacy, and charm of her normal speech.

What was her obstacle? Suspecting misdirected effort, I interrupted her reading:

Coach: *Can I suggest a change in plans?*

Brenda: *Oh, sure.*

Coach: *You know this story, right?*

Brenda: *Sorta, kinda.*

Coach: *What's it about?*

Brenda: *It's about a man who lives in New York City and wants to change the attitudes of people in New York City.*

Coach: *Uh-huh.*

Brenda: *And what he does is, he goes to spread his good will by spreading pleasant words to everybody he meets.*

At this point, Brenda began to tell her story fluently and engrossingly—unaware that she was doing more than telling us "about" her story. I listened with delight to her entire performance.

Clearly, Brenda knew this story much better than she thought. She had experienced the story well enough—and knew enough about how to tell a story—to do much more than read it.

Her primary obstacle was therefore not needing experience of the story, nor was it lack of information.

When asked to *tell* a story, she was unable. When asked to *tell about* a story, she was able to tell it with clarity and passion. Therefore, she had some misconception about what it means to *tell* a story. To determine what her misconception was, I asked her a question:

Coach: *That was lovely. How would it have been different, if you had actually told it?*

Brenda: *Oh, it would have had a lot more to it. I left out a lot of the details.*

Brenda's reply showed where she was mistaken. Her telling "about" the story actually had *more* details—both in words and in gestures—than the written version.

Like many of us schooled to memorize words on a page, Brenda thought that telling a story is something like reading without the paper. She thought if she did not know every word on the paper, she could not tell the story right. Further, she did not recognize the intricacy of oral communication. Thus, she focused on her leaving out some of the words, but did not notice that she knew—and added zest to—the story.

Brenda's misconception, therefore, is about what it means to tell a story. Until she came to understand her misconception, she would continue to put effort into getting the words right, instead of into getting the story right.

After I mentioned how well she had done, she gave me an opportunity to correct her misconception:

Brenda: *I kind of gave you the gist of it all, kind of took things away from the original story. Hopefully gave you the same meaning as the original story.*

Coach: *I think so!*

Brenda: *With the same feeling ...*

Coach: *I think so!*

Brenda: *... that it gives me.*

Coach: *That's all there is. That's it. That's telling stories. There's no more to it than that.*

Brenda: *OK.*

Coach: *You don't have to do anything different from that. The thing that you think you have to do is a fiction. That was a beautiful telling! You told it really simply, really from your heart. You added lots of wonderful details.*

Brenda: *I think sometimes that you think you have to have those actual words that were on paper, in print—but you don't.*

Coach: *You don't. In fact, they would get in the way. They have nothing to do with storytelling. What you just did is just right!*

Brenda has finally noticed what she was trying to do, and that another approach is possible. Now she will be able to approach stories directly, without misdirecting her effort toward memorizing verbal details.

As coach, first I noticed her misdirected effort, then I diagnosed its cause as a misconception about storytelling in general. At that point I didn't just tell her what was wrong. Instead, I found a way to get Brenda to experience telling the story without laboring to remember it exactly. Then, after she had succeeded, I explained to her what she had just done.

Often, in the case of misdirected effort, the challenge to my creativity is to find a way to circumvent your misconception, so that you can experience success. It often takes several tries to get you to stop what you think you should be doing long enough for you to notice the easier way.

Incidentally, I might have looked at Brenda and thought that her lack of confidence was the obstacle. But such an approach would deal with the symptom, not the cause. Her lack of confidence in this case was caused by her misconception about needing to know every word.

Taking self-confidence as the obstacle, I might even have been able to help Brenda tell more confidently. But she still would have been "reading" from an imaginary paper, not speaking from her own internalized experience of the story. She still would have been misdirecting her effort.

Charming the Audience

Establishing rapport with your listeners is an essential part of telling them stories or convincing them to fund your project or vote for your point of view. Yet you may continue to put effort into gaining the audience's interest or approval long after it is appropriate.

MAKING US TAKE YOU SERIOUSLY

June told a Native American story about sharing the earth's resources. Her introduction began this way:

The story I want to tell you today symbolizes greed, and I think it personifies a lot of what I feel about what is going on with regard to the rain forests. The people are fighting very hard to save the rain forests from the greed of agribusiness ....

She ended her story with these words:

Some of the people were so happy, they dove down into the bottom of the river and they turned into fishes and turtles—and there they live until this day.

And no one, but no one can ever own the waters of the world. We have to share them, because no one has the right to say, "This is my water and not yours."

The story itself left me feeling united with my fellow creatures and determined to treat the earth as everyone's. The introduction and the last paragraph, on the other hand, left me feeling preached at. Naturally, this made me feel defensive, and made it more difficult for me to open up to her story. Thus, June's actual story was working, but her introduction and last paragraph were getting in the way.

During appreciations, many participants mentioned June's obvious passion for the subject matter, and shared the messages about the environment that her story had conveyed to them. When time came for suggestions, I asked June what the story meant to her. She repeated the gist of her introduction, then added, "I am so emotionally involved in the history of environmentalism, I hope I don't turn into one of these emotional activists on stage, throwing my message out to people. I'd love comments about that."

At this point, I knew her goals for the story, and her fear that she would be "preachy." I also knew that her introduction—an explicit statement of her goals—was, in fact, more preachy than she wanted it to be.

I guessed that an unconscious misconception lay behind her preachiness. She was aware of being preachy, but she was not aware of what caused her to apply the effort that came out as preachiness. I asked her a question.

Coach: *Did you notice that we got from your story what you wanted us to get?*

June: *Well, yes. I guess so.*

Coach: Look *around at the group. Remember what people said they learned.*

June: *You're right. It was even more than I hoped for.*

Coach: *What would it be like, if you knew we would understand the importance of your story—if you knew that even before you started?*

June: *I guess I'd relax.*

Coach: *How about the introduction?*

June: *You mean, it gets in the way.*

Coach: *I think you might be trying to force us to see how meaningful your story is when we don't need to be forced.*

June: *Probably. Yes.*

Coach: *You can think of your job as assuming that we will find this story just as important as you find it. From that place, you won't have to worry about throwing your message at us.*

June: *I see. Just offer it to you unadorned.*

June added unnecessary interpretations of her story because she assumed unconsciously that we would not otherwise take her story seriously. Once she became aware of this assumption, she could put her effort into "offering it unadorned."

Until June could see where she was trying too hard, she would continue her attempt. If I said, "Omit the introduction," she would have found some other way to convince us of the story's significance—if not through extra words, then through "elevated" tone of voice or solemn gestures and facial expressions.

MAKING US LIKE YOU

Pauline told a long fairytale that left us spellbound. As a listener, I felt myself nourished by her story. She led me on a dream-like journey below the surface of my mind.

Yet something bothered me. As she guided me on this imagination journey, Pauline seemed frequently to want something from me. I felt pulled to respond to her in a way that distracted me slightly from the story.

When it was time for suggestions, I was unable to identify the exact problem. Therefore, I asked her to repeat a part of her story, a part that had bothered me. After a minute or two, I saw what Pauline was doing that did not belong in her story:

Pauline: *The hag sucked up the food into her huge mouth ...*

Coach: *Wait a second! Why are you smiling?*

Pauline: *I'm not conscious of smiling.*

Coach: *Do you feel nervous?*

Pauline: *I don't know why the smile is there. I was not conscious of being nervous at all.*

Coach: *What it seems like you're doing is, you are soothing us, charming us. I almost think we'd have to watch a video of yourself telling, then I could say, "There—do you see that?" It's below the level of awareness.*

Pauline: *It's a smile that's extraneous to the story.*

Coach: *It's not part of the story at all, in fact. It's part of your interaction with us. There is a piece in which you need us to reassure you. Does that ring true in any way?*

Pauline: *Yes.*

Coach: *You're good at charming us. The charm is fine. But you've got to decide who it's for. If it's for us, fine. If it's for you, then maybe you should respond differently to your need.*

At this point, I've identified what Pauline was doing that seemed dissonant: she was smiling at me in a way that made me feel I was supposed to smile back. I have also told her my hypothesis about why she was doing it: to get us to tell her that she was doing OK.

Assuming that she comes to agree with my perceptions, I still need to give her a new place in which to direct her effort:

Coach: *Do you remember a moment during your story when you felt sure that we were completely into the story?*

Pauline: *When the soldier was about to trick the hag.*

Coach: *How did you know we were into the story?*

Pauline: *I could just feel that you were with me.*

Coach: *Great! My suggestion is that before you even begin the story, you imagine that you already have the feeling that we are with you. Provide that feeling for yourself. The truth of the matter is, when you don't try to charm us, you're even more delightful.*

Without her unnecessary efforts to get us to assure her, Pauline will be free to direct all of her considerable skills toward the charms of her story.

STOPPING THE DOWNWARD SPIRAL

Both June and Pauline directed unnecessary effort toward getting us, their audience, to respond to them. In both cases, I recommended that they begin by imagining for themselves the result they wanted.

Whenever you are misdirecting effort in order to get a response from the audience, your efforts almost always have the opposite effect. They can therefore start a downward spiral: you feel us slipping away, and apply more effort in the same direction.

Only you can stop this spiral. You can decide not to pursue the response at all, or you can imagine that you have already achieved it. Either way, you can redirect your effort more profitably.

Avoiding Feelings

Sometimes you misdirect your efforts in order to avoid an unpleasant feeling. On the one hand, the feeling may be about the act of performing (or writing or sculpting) itself. On the other hand, the feeling may be about the particular story you are telling (or the article you are writing or the statue you are carving).

ROCKING THE ARK

When Abby told her version of "Noah's Ark," the coaching workshop members responded with enthusiasm. Her simple, personal telling made the familiar story seem individually relevant to each of us.

During the suggestion period, one participant mentioned that Abby seemed to rock back and forth on her feet. Abby responded, "I'll try to be aware of that."

Knowing that trying to be aware of a bad habit often ties up awareness better saved for other purposes, I interrupted:

Coach: *Abby, would you like help with the rocking?*
Abby: *Sure.*
Coach: *Tell me the beginning again.*

As Abby told, I stood next to her. As soon as she began to rock, I steadied her with my hand.

Coach: *Notice what it feels like to want to rock.*
Abby: *I'm just wondering what you're going to do next.*

I interpreted Abby's remark to mean that my physical presence was distracting to her. This approach was not working. Time to try another one!

Coach: *I'll sit back down. Let's try something else. Try standing there like Noah himself, inviting the animals onto the Ark.*

Abby: *Well, I'd stand more like this. [Plants feet more widely, spreads arms as though welcoming.]*

Coach: *How does that feel?*

Abby: *It feels scary. Visible.*

This new approach was paying off. My hypothesis was now that Abby was rocking because standing still made her feel visible—and this feeling was frightening to her. If her obstacle was effort directed into avoiding that feeling, she might be able to simply welcome the feeling instead.

Coach: *Do you know how powerful your story was? How much it meant to the people here?*

Abby: *Yes. I heard them.*

Coach: *Can you claim a space for that story, knowing how important it is to people?*

Abby: Yes. It means that much to me, too.

Coach: *Try telling the beginning again, in that stance, claiming a space like Noah telling the animals how to be safe in the flood.*

When Abby retold the opening of her story, not only did she not rock in place, she told it even more forcefully.

Coach: *That was even better than before. When you feel that, when you really give yourself permission to take charge of your space, then you don't need to rock.*

Abby: *So true!*

When she was unconsciously avoiding the feeling of being visible, Abby fidgeted. Once she redirected her effort toward claiming a visible space for her story, however, she stood as solid as Mount Ararat.

If Abby had settled for her first resolution to "try to be aware of" her rocking, she would have had to split her attention: part of it would be on what she was communicating, while part of it would remind her not to rock. With her new focus on claiming her space, in contrast, her stance becomes an integral part of her passion for sharing her story.

✧ COVERING THE MOON ON HER FOREHEAD ✧

There was once a beautiful woman who was born with the shining shape of a crescent moon on her forehead. Everywhere she went, people commented on this unique feature. All through her life, the moon on her forehead assured her of praise and admiration.

In time, however, she wished to enter the world of deeper learning. She went to the Master Teacher of the land, and asked to become her disciple.

The Master Teacher refused her. When the beautiful woman asked why, she was told, "You devote too much attention to the moon on your forehead."

Suddenly, the beautiful woman saw how vain she was. Determined to make a complete change in her life, she covered the shining moon with mud. Lest anyone be attracted to her by its light, she carried extra mud at all times, and a mirror to check frequently that the moon on her forehead was discreetly covered.

After many months, she returned to the Master Teacher, asking again to be taken as a disciple.

This time the Master Teacher said, "Certainly not. Now the moon on your forehead consumes even more of your attention than before!"

JUMPING TO A CONCLUSION

Jay spent months developing the first draft of a story about his Uncle Mark, a reclusive old man who had fascinated Jay as a child.

After many sessions of exploratory talking, scene-creating, and trial performances, Jay performed for me an eighty-minute draft of the story.

Several scenes had a mysterious power that I knew related to his goal for his story. Several others, however, had a different character. They were clever and interesting, but they seemed to lack the dark attraction of the other scenes. Somehow, they felt less like comic relief than like distractions.

Having coached Jay for many years, I did not need to lead him through the process as carefully as I would lead someone I just met. Nonetheless, I did need to confirm my perceptions of the powerful scenes. During the appreciation section of his session, I listed the images that seemed powerful to me. When it came time for suggestions, I told him my perceptions:

Coach: *The scenes I mentioned before seem like they approach the core of your story. Is that right?*

Jay: *Absolutely. Those are the ones that draw me to them.*

Coach: *I get the feeling that you created these other scenes* [lists them] *in order to stitch the story together, and make it seem more complete. Is that right?*

Jay: *Yes. I was being a tailor and sewing it all together.*

Coach: *I think it's too soon to start stitching. You still don't know what kind of a garment you're making.*

Jay: *You're right.*

Coach: *For now, keep letting the images develop. Just tell the parts that move you, whether they make sense together or not. You can do the sewing together later on, once the shape has started to emerge.*

Jay: *Developing, not sewing! That was very helpful.*

As I confirmed with Jay later, he was feeling afraid that his story would never take shape. To avoid that fear, he misdirected effort into "sewing" the story together. Thus, his obstacle was misdirecting effort to avoid a feeling.

The assistance he needed that week was just a reminder to keep his attention on exploring those mysterious images—the images that form the core of the story he was trying to create.

Tools for Helping

The examples in this chapter illustrate the general principle for helping you overcome your misdirected effort: I must help you rescind your decision to apply the effort.

I have several basic tools for applying this principle. First, I can help you notice your effort. Second, I can help you experience what it is like to tell without applying the effort. Third, I can give you a substitute effort to apply.

NOTICE YOUR EFFORT

If you can notice the unproductive effort you are applying, you will probably be able to stop applying it.

"Noticing your effort" means becoming conscious of applying the effort, not "noticing its effects." Abby ("Rocking the Ark," page 146), for example, was aware of her rocking (the effect of her effort) before she became aware of her effort not to feel visible.

One simple way to help you notice your effort is to ask you why you are doing something. I asked Pauline ("Making Us Like You," page 144), "Why are you smiling?"

If it doesn't work to ask you directly, I can sometimes describe what your effort appears to be. In Jay's session ("Jumping to a Conclusion," page 148), I said, "I get the feeling that you created these scenes in order to stitch the story together .... Is that right?"

I may need to make several attempts before I describe your effort in terms that make sense to you. In Pauline's session, she couldn't answer my question about smiling. So I asked, "Do you feel nervous?" When she answered in the negative, I went on to describe the effect she seemed to be trying for. I said, "What it seems like you're doing is, you are soothing us, charming us ....There is a piece in which you need us to reassure you." This turned out to be the effort that she could recognize—and therefore cease.

In my own case ("My Evil Landowner," page 137), my coach asked me, "Is there a part of you that is like that landowner?" This question directed my attention to the connection between me and the landowner character. Once I put my attention on that connection, I noticed that I had been putting effort into disrupting it.

Getting you to notice your effort is a direct approach to your obstacle, but it does not always work. Sometimes my attempt to call attention to your effort is distracting in itself, as when my presence next to Abby made it hard for her to answer the query, "Notice what it feels like not to rock." More commonly, you are simply not able to notice your unconscious effort directly. In this case, I must use other approaches.

EXPERIENCE THE ABSENCE OF YOUR EFFORT

Since your misdirected effort is usually unconscious and habitual, you may not be able to stop applying it at will or even to notice it.

If you cannot notice your effort, I can try to help you experience the *absence* of your effort. For example, you may have experienced a moment in which you did not apply your effort. If so, I can call your attention to what that moment felt like. Or you may be able—with my help—to imagine a situation in which you *would not* apply the effort. Alternatively, I can set up a special exercise in the hopes that it will allow you to experience the absence of the effort.

If you have already experienced the lack of effort at some point in your telling, I can try to identify that point. Thus, I asked Pauline, "Do you remember a moment during your story when you felt sure that we were completely into the story?" This would likely be a moment when she did not feel the need to charm us further. By calling her attention to her feelings at that moment, I could ask her to tell the entire story as though she were feeling that way—that is, without applying effort to charm us.

Even if you did not experience a single moment without your misdirected effort, you may be able to imagine not applying the effort. I asked June ("Making Us Take You Seriously," page 142), "What would it be like if you knew we would understand the importance of your story—if you knew that even before you started?" Her reply, "I guess I'd relax," suggested that she had successfully imagined not having to convince us of her story's importance.

Sometimes I need to set up a situation in which you will not apply the effort. Afterwards, I can ask you to notice what it felt like *not* to apply it.

In Brenda's session ("Misconceptions About Performance," page 139), I asked her to tell me what her story was about. Brenda's obstacle was an unconscious misconception about performing stories that led her to focus on getting every detail correct. Since this was not a "performance," however, she did not focus on the details; she told her story without bothering to misapply effort. After this success I could say, "You don't have to do anything different from that. The thing you think you have to do is a fiction."

If none of these approaches work, I may be able to "trick" your effort by having you apply its opposite. This works best when you are applying effort to prevent something. Gordon, for example, rushed through his story without pausing. When asked why, he said, "I guess I'm afraid of being boring." Then I asked him to tell the same story in the most boring way possible. The result was neither boring nor rushed. By applying an opposite effort, he succeeded in neutralizing his usual effort. By allowing himself to be boring, he experienced telling a story without misdirected effort to prevent boredom.

Setting up such a situation has an element of deceit in it—necessarily. If I told you in advance what I was doing, you would probably continue to apply your usual misdirected effort. To minimize any diminution of trust caused by my trickery, I make sure to begin such an exercise with a request to try something different and unspecified. In Brenda's case, I asked, "Can I suggest a change in plans?" Other times I say something like, "Are you willing to try something?"

Direct Your Effort Elsewhere

If you think, "I shouldn't scratch my nose," the urge to do so magnifies. One way to avoid this phenomenon is to substitute a positive commandment for a negative one. This is similar to preventing yourself from thinking of a pink elephant by thinking of a blue mouse instead.

Even when you have already succeeded in noticing your effort and ceasing it, it may help to find a substitute effort to apply. Thus, in my "evil landowner" session, I determined to connect with the evil in myself. In her session, Brenda learned to "give you the gist of it all ... to give you the same meaning as the original story." June left her session determined to "offer the story unadorned." Pauline's new focus was to "imagine you have the feeling we are with you." Jay went home with the intention of letting the images develop.

Even if you can't notice your effort or experience its absence, it may work for you to find a new effort to apply. Abby only confronted the feeling she was avoiding after she discovered her "Noah stance," which was her new focus of attention.

Avoiding Harm

I face two special dangers in helping you overcome misdirected effort. I may add to your misconceptions, and I may leave you feeling hopeless.

✧ BOY SEEKS DOG ✧

Once there was a boy who grew up in a village that had no animals. One day, a bully from a neighboring village called the boy "a worthless dog."

The boy asked his father, "What is a dog?"

The father said, "A dog is about knee high, and has four legs and fur."

"But father, why would that bully call me a dog?"

"Only out of ignorance. Now leave me to do my work."

The boy thought, "I will show that ignorant bully what a dog is, and then he'll know I am not a dog." So he searched his village for something knee-high with four legs and fur.

Seeing a low table, he thought, "This is almost a dog; it lacks only the fur." He covered the tabletop with fur and took it to his busy father.

"Father, is this a dog?"

"No, son. A dog is an animal. It moves on its own."

Never having seen an animal, the boy began looking for a low, furry table that moved on its own. At last, he added wheels to his table and returned to his father.

"Father, is this a dog?"

Without turning to look, the father asked, "Does it have a tail and a bark? Then it is not a dog."

Interpreting the words "bark" and "tail" in light of his concept of a dog, the boy added a tree-bark edging to his table and made up a "tale" about it, then returned to his busy father.

"No, son. A dog is alive!"

At last the boy understood that he would never find a dog in his village.

He went out into the world, seeking a low, furry, bark-edged, tale-honored table—that was alive.

One day, in a far-off land, a dog crossed his path. He asked a passerby to name the creature he had seen. Only then did he learn what a dog was.

ADDING TO YOUR MISCONCEPTION

When your obstacle is lack of information, the most helpful thing I can do is to give you the information you need.

When your obstacle is needing more experience of the story (or any presentation or project), information from me will not help you, but it will probably not make your obstacle more difficult.

When your obstacle is misdirected effort, however, there is a substantial danger that information from me will *add* to your obstacle. When dealing with unconscious effort, restricting our work to the conscious realm is ineffective—like trying to rebuild a house without fixing the foundation.

As Rhonda told her story, she bobbed her head constantly while she scanned the room from one side to the other—almost as though she were counting the audience members over and over. After I asked her several questions, she revealed to me that a previous instructor had told her to make eye contact with her audience. This constant movement was her interpretation of what she had been told to do.

The instructor had failed to notice Rhonda's misdirected effort, and, in fact, had added to it. He had noticed Rhonda's failure to look at her audience as she told her story, and had given information that said, in effect, "Good storytellers make eye contact with their audience."

Like Abby, Rhonda was avoiding the feeling of being visible. Given the advice about eye contact, she found a way to make "eye contact" without feeling visible. She added the new advice to her unconscious effort, resulting in effort that was even more unproductive.

I helped Rhonda notice her original effort to avoid being visible, then helped her redirect it. The new direction that proved workable for her was to try to connect with her audience—which she accomplished flexibly through appropriate eye contact as well as through other means.

LEAVING YOU HOPELESS

Since your misdirected effort is usually unconscious and beyond your direct control, I run the risk of leaving you with the feeling that your storytelling has a defect that you have no hope of correcting.

Years ago, I told a story about a group of lumberjacks teasing a newcomer. I went to a coach who noticed—accurately—that my portrayal of the old-timers lacked force.

I know now that I was misdirecting effort, by trying not to be a bully. This effort had nothing to do with storytelling; since childhood I had tried not to be one of the "mean men." Until I could redirect this effort, no other effort could succeed in making these characters sound convincing.

The coach asked me to portray the lumberjacks with more force. Of course, they became forceful, but not in a way that fit the situation. After a few more frustrating attempts, the coach gave up.

So did I.

I left that coaching session with two thoughts: first, I was doing something wrong with those characters; second, I had no idea what it was or how to correct it. I felt defective and hopeless. I lost all desire to tell that story. Even worse, I internalized the notion that I was inherently unable to portray forceful men.

Years later, I was able to notice and cease my effort to "not be a bad man." Then I was able to portray forceful men easily and flexibly.

Knowing When Not to Try

If I don't have the time, the skill, or the willingness to work with you in depth about your misdirected effort, it's usually better not to bring it up.

After all, there's always another coach and another day. But if you give up in discouragement, you'll never find that other coach.

It's fine for me to leave you with work to do. There's no harm in leaving you knowing that you need information, experience of your story, or help with misdirected effort. The harm comes when I leave you feeling defective or powerless.

To avoid this harm, I can remember several principles.

I can notice your misdirected effort, and try not to confuse it with other obstacles.

I can remember the kind of frustration that sometimes arises when working on misdirected effort, and avoid naming the symptoms of your effort in a way that leaves you with no hope of improving.

I can remain humble, vulnerable, and respectful. I can remember my own struggles with similar obstacles. When I fail to help you, I can admit it and change course. I can check with you before each step of tackling your misdirected effort.

I can hold out hope. I can relate examples of storytellers or other presenters—including myself—who have overcome similar obstacles. I can forcefully state my appreciations of your story. I can refer you to other coaches whom I respect.

I can remind us both of the first principle of good coaching: I believe in your success.

Coaching to Overcome The Fourth Obstacle: Emotional Blocks

The first three kinds of obstacles represent various difficulties, mostly in the cognitive realm. The fourth kind of obstacle, however, has less to do with information, meaning, and effort, and more to do with feelings; it represents a blockage purely in the emotional realm.

Entering the emotional realm is uncomfortable for some presenters and some coaches. The reason to enter it, of course, is that feelings are sometimes your obstacle. You and I have no choice about what your obstacle is, but we *can* decide whether to work together in this realm. (For more on the decision to work with feelings, see "Should I Deal With Feelings At All?" page 174.)

Sometimes your obstacle will arise from feelings about telling stories (or making presentations) in general, as when you feel anxiety about telling any story in front of a group. Other times, your feelings will relate to the content of a particular story.

The Presence of Sadness

Doris came to a coaching workshop with a Jewish folktale about Elijah—who is often portrayed in Jewish lore as traveling about in disguise, bringing blessings to the worthy. In this story, Elijah rewards a generous but poor couple with seven years of wealth. At the end of the seven years, Elijah sees they have become stingy, and removes his blessing, thus sending them back into poverty.

Doris's performance was straightforward and unemotional. I assumed that she saw the story as a moral lesson about stinginess. Fortunately, I decided to test my assumption before venturing any suggestions:

Coach: *What draws you to this story?*

Doris: *It's the way the couple lived—how sad it was.*

Coach: *Tell me about the sad part.*

Doris: *I think that the money made them shrink up inside, and that's so sad for me.*

Whoa! I had been completely wrong about her goals. I needed to understand more clearly what she wanted to have happen in the story. It was time for more questions:

Coach: *So, you see them as more joyful at the start ...*

Doris: *They are happy! They give what little they have away, just for the joy of it.*

Coach: ... *and then, over the seven years, they lose that happiness. Why?*

Doris: *They think they have to protect the money he gave them. They cut off their own joy. They die, spiritually.*

Coach: *And the story ends in sadness, is that right?*

Doris: *Yes.*

Now that I had an idea of what Doris was trying for, I could compare it with what she actually achieved. The divergence was quite great.

Clearly, there was a major obstacle. What was it?

She might have needed information about how to give her story the emotional shape she wanted.

She might also have needed more experience of the story. She was very clear about the story's overall shape and meaning, but she might have needed to imagine the crucial scenes more fully.

She might easily have been misdirecting effort in a way that was constricting the story's emotional dimension.

How could I know which potential obstacle was actually in the way?

Comparing her goals with her actual performance, I noticed that the missing element was the central feeling: the sadness. I decided to put her attention toward letting the sadness be present in the story, then to see if an obstruction came up:

Coach: *How could we get some of that sadness in the story?*

Doris: *You mean, emote about it?*

Coach: *No, just let it be there. I think it might belong in the story.*

Doris was quiet for a moment, evidently imagining the sadness in the story. Then she began to cry.

As soon as she started crying, I thought I recognized her obstacle—which was not one of the three I had considered. Rather than interpret her crying as a symptom of her frustration with the coaching process or of how tired she was that day, I took her crying as release of emotional tension about the content of her story. In order to let the sadness inhabit her story, I hypothesized, she needed to come to terms with an emotional block.

Acting on this hypothesis, I stood quietly and confidently next to her, letting her cry. After a few minutes, she seemed done crying, so I said:

Coach: *Do you want to try to tell part of it again, now?*

Doris: *Yes.*

Her new telling—in almost the same words as her first telling—had a depth of feeling that was completely missing earlier. Whatever internal process had accompanied her tears, it had allowed the central emotion to enter her story, just as she had desired. She had overcome the obstacle that was blocking the sadness.

THREE WAYS TO OVERCOME

Like Doris, you may find yourself at one time or another facing blocked emotion. How you overcome this obstacle depends on many factors.

You have three basic choices, however.

You can, in some cases, simply decide to give yourself access to the blocked feelings. In other cases, like Doris's, you will need to release some emotional tension. In still other cases, you will make a decision to act, not on your feelings, but on your awareness of the current situation. Often, you will combine two or all three of these methods.

Let the Feelings In

Once, I was polishing an Appalachian folktale, "Jack and the Bull," for a radio broadcast. I told it to a coach who said, "The entire story was wonderful! My only suggestion has to do with the scenes where Jack is in the tree watching his bull as it fights those other animals. Those scenes seem flat. What's going on there?"

I was surprised by her response. After all, I had been telling the story for years, and had never noticed any flagging of audience interest.

I took a deep breath, then mentally reviewed the scenes she mentioned. As I imagined each scene, I paid attention to my feelings. Using her helpful direction of "What's going on?" I surveyed my emotions and bodily sensations.

As I expected, there were no surprises.

Oops! Wait a minute.

My thoughts went to a period of my childhood when some adults close to me had several arguments that had frightened me. Why was I remembering that period?

A moment later, it became clear to me. Jack's helpless witnessing of his beloved bull's fights reminded me—until that moment, unconsciously—of my own experiences watching helplessly while the adults around me argued.

At all times, we have sensations that we are attentive to, judging them to be relevant to the task at hand, and other sensations that we ignore as irrelevant. As I sit writing these words, I can feel the chair on my legs and my clothes against my skin. Until I decided to let those sensations in, I was unaware of them; they were irrelevant to my writing. Nonetheless, I have the ability to tune them in at any time.

My emotions about the arguments I witnessed as a child were in a similar state of suppression. Long ago, I made an unconscious decision to stop feeling the helpless feelings of those childhood evenings. Periodically, of course, some event or image would bring them up more strongly than usual. These helpless feelings would call for my attention like a phone ringing on a private line. I had grown so used to ignoring that particular "ring," however, that I didn't always weigh consciously whether to "answer the phone" or not. This "phone" was "ringing" while I told my story, but I had screened it out as irrelevant.

My coach's query made me notice the feelings and realize that they were, in fact, highly relevant.

At this point, I retold those sections of my story for her, making only one change: I allowed myself to feel my childhood feelings as I described the actions of the tale. After my retelling, my coach said, "That telling was completely different. Whatever you did differently fixed the problem."

What I had done differently was to remove an emotional block. The relevant feelings had been available to me, but habitually blocked. In this example, to overcome the obstacle I needed only to become aware of the feelings, then to decide to let the feelings into my awareness.

Heal the Hurt

When we are hurt physically, we spontaneously heal. In the same way, when we are hurt emotionally—due to grief, fear, embarrassment, or other emotional pain—we spontaneously heal. The physical healing process is typically accompanied by increased blood flow, swelling, and other indications. The emotional healing process is typically accompanied by such indications as tears, shaking, laughter, perspiration, or animated talking.

We can cause the physical healing process to be postponed for a short time. If my life is in danger, the increased blood flow to the large wound on my leg does not start until I've outrun the saber-toothed tiger who bit me. I have reduced functioning, however, until I actually heal; my wounded leg won't carry me as well as a healed leg.

We can postpone the emotional healing process, too, but for much longer periods. If the saber-toothed tiger that scared me is prowling near my cave, I can keep from crying until the tiger leaves. And if my companions tell me that crying is only for sissies, I can continue to postpone the healing process for years.

The cost of living with unhealed emotional hurts is reduced functioning, just as with unhealed physical hurts. Unhealed emotional hurts can hamper our ability to imagine, to absorb information, and to respond to new information appropriately.

For example, someone who has finished the process of grieving for a loved one (healed the emotional hurt from the loss) can think easily about pleasant memories of the loved one, and can even describe the loved one's death with relaxed clarity. Before the hurt has healed, however, even pleasant memories may seem too painful to imagine. Whole areas of the person's life may be too closely associated with the loss of the loved one to think about. New information that reminds the person of the loved one may seem too painful to absorb. The person may respond to new situations as though they, too, are painful, if they bring up associations with the ungrieved loss.

Similar loss of functioning can happen even with less traumatic emotional hurts, until the hurts are healed. A character who reminds you of an annoying co-worker may be difficult for you to imagine fully if you have not had a chance to talk or laugh about the co-worker's actions.

In a storytelling performance, unhealed emotional hurts can impair our ability to imagine or think about our story. (They can just as easily impair our ability to think about a problem or a project.) Or they can hinder us from expressing a feeling we have imagined. Or they can lead us to express an inappropriate feeling. In other cases, they can prevent us from connecting with our audience, customers, or co-workers.

Throughout this book, I use "emotional hurt" to signify what is sometimes called "trauma" or "acute psychological stress." I use "unhealed emotional hurt" to refer to what is variously known as "unresolved feelings," "psychological baggage," or "old tapes."

Whatever one calls these problems that all of us carry with us, they tend to surface until they are addressed. Once they are fully addressed ("healed," in my terminology) they no longer pull at our attention or block our ability to think. At this point, when the subject of the trauma is no longer problematic, we are in an ideal position to deal creatively and forcefully with this very subject in our artwork, stories, or other communications.

TRY OUT BEING AFRAID

I was teaching a class of seventh graders to tell the stories they had collected from their families. Brad got up to tell his story to the class, then suddenly said, "I forgot my story."

Trying to put Brad at ease, I said, "Take your time. Take as long as you need." He responded by looking more ill at ease than before. He turned to me, then glanced at his audience. Now he looked afraid.

I guessed that Brad, like many people, was feeling embarrassed or frightened when confronted with a group of listeners.

Fear is useful: it helps us survive danger, in part by making us forget everything unrelated to our immediate survival. Less forceful feelings like embarrassment and fear of humiliation also have the power to commandeer our attention.

Brad's embarrassment, I concluded, made him forget the story that he knew so well a moment before.

If Brad had actually been in danger, his fear would have been appropriate. As it was, however, he was not even in danger of criticism—there was a supportive atmosphere in the classroom, his classmates were sympathetic and had agreed to be helpful listeners, and I was there to monitor their responses. Therefore, Brad's fear was a sign of a previous emotional hurt that had not yet healed. He had an emotional block.

Clearly, his problem was very different from mine when telling "Jack and the Bull." I had been unconsciously cutting off my feelings; he was painfully, debilitatingly aware of his fear. A different sort of help was needed.

I decided to try helping him heal some of his painful feelings, right there. Knowing that it is "uncool" among Brad's peers to show fear, however, I knew that the display of feelings that accompanies the healing of embarrassment would probably bring with it more embarrassment. One way out of that quandary would be to make everyone show the feeling at once:

Coach: *Are you willing to try something?*

Brad: *Sure.*

Coach: *Let's have everyone do this with us. Will you all please stand up where you are? Now, everyone do this with me.*

At this point, I led the entire class in an exaggerated parody of fear. We all spent thirty seconds shaking and sounding terrified. Many of us, including Brad, giggled with embarrassment.

Before the class could even sit back down, Brad began his story. He told it all, confidently and well.

I believe that Brad's laughter during that thirty seconds was the outward indication of the healing of some of his fears and embarrassment. Once he had healed some emotional hurt, it was no longer commandeering all his attention. He had overcome the emotional block that was preventing him from remembering his story.

I was struck by how quickly Brad returned to his story, and by his apparent lack of desire to talk about his feelings, even as they healed. Like many adults, I tend to favor talking as a form of healing emotional hurt, sincle talking is usually considered more acceptable than laughing, shaking, or crying. But Brad was able to make better use of laughter than of words. In my role as coach, I tried to offer him the form of healing that he seemed best able to use, not the form with which I felt most comfortable.

Brad's return to telling his story was sudden. When I am healing my own emotional hurt, I usually require a more gradual transition from healing to functioning. As a result, I was prepared to allow him to take a few transitional minutes. Once Brad was ready to return to telling his story, however, I had no reason to insist on a more gradual process.

PUSH THROUGH THE ANGER

Gail stood up in front of a coaching workshop and introduced her story about Miriam, the Jewish prophet. She described her reaction to hearing, as an adult, the full story of Miriam. She was outraged: why hadn't she been told such stories of strong women when she was a child? Her outrage had led her to begin storytelling, so she could make sure that others heard these important stories.

Next, Gail told the story. It had power, but was told in an emotional monotone.

What was her obstacle? What was preventing her from telling her story with the same emotional ebb and flow with which she had told her introduction.

I suspected an emotional block. She had told of her outrage, with appropriate affect. Her performance, however, felt as though her outrage remained present, even in parts of the story that were tender or triumphant. Was she unable to "turn off" her outrage?

I tried helping her heal some of her hurt. In front of the group, I asked her to push her hands against mine. As she pushed, I asked her to say, with righteous indignation, "Why didn't you tell me?" As she began, her face and neck grew red. I took this as the outward sign of the healing of righteous anger. After a few minutes of pushing with my repeated encouragement, the red subsided from her face. She said, "That felt good."

I asked her to begin her story again. This time, she told it with emotional flexibility. Without losing its power, the story had gained shape and grace.

With my help, Gail had expressed and thereby released some

of her unresolved anger. Her expression of righteous indignation had allowed the release of emotional tension, much as tears allow the release of grief. She may have had more anger yet to heal, but for the moment her anger was no longer a constant force that intruded on her story. It was available to her to feel, but it was not drowning out her other feelings. By resolving some of her past conflict, she had overcome her emotional block.

Remember the Current Reality

In some cases, you may be able to overcome an emotional block by deciding to be aware of certain feelings.

In other cases, you may be able to heal some emotional hurts within your coaching session, thereby dissolving some or all of the block.

In many cases, however, another strategy will be most efficient: to focus your attention on the reality of your current situation.

The current situation for a storyteller is usually quite safe, compared with how afraid you might feel. Very few storytellers have actually been tarred and feathered or assassinated while on the job. Very few of the hostile fans who sometimes sneak into professional soccer arenas attend storytelling events. The listeners who attend a storytelling event may even share your interest in stories and their power. Most audiences want to be entertained and moved; therefore, they want you to succeed.

Feelings that interfere with your storytelling are—in virtually every case—not appropriate to the present situation. They were probably once appropriate to an emotionally hurtful situation, but, because they have not healed, they persist even though circumstances have changed.

A powerful tool for dealing with these old emotional hurts is to notice how the current situation differs from the old situation. Although you may feel afraid, for example, you may not be in danger right now. Although you may feel angry, there may not be someone infringing on you at this moment. Although you may feel powerless, you may actually be able to get whatever you need at the moment.

There are three major ways to remind yourself that things have changed. You can focus on an image. You can focus on a statement about the current situation. Or you can take action that provides a corrective experience.

FIND A CORRECTIVE IMAGE

At a coaching workshop, Rebecca gave a first telling of what she called a parable. She told of an unhappy, quarrelsome village that was about to be invaded by boatfuls of terrible monsters—who turned out to be nothing more than babies cast adrift by the last survivor of a flooded village in order to save the babies' lives. Once the unhappy villagers realized who the invaders were, they treated them with love and nurturing. After this experience, they treated all strangers—and each other—like babies. From that time on, harmony was restored in the village.

This was how she began:

"Well (shrugs), this is kind of a parable more than any kind of a folktale. So, once there was a village by the sea. And the people were in a panic. A messenger had just arrived by canoe bearing terrible news: the boats of mysterious invaders (giggles, shrugs) were making their way with the tides down the coast. Already, the messenger said, the two villages to the north were abandoned. The invaders, known only as the Gagars, would be upon them by morning. (Shrugs.) Uh, anyway ...."

Rebecca's non-verbal cues (giggles and shrugs) were making me feel uneasy and were distracting me from her piece. It seemed as though something was distracting her from her story, too.

What was interfering?

After Rebecca finished her story, she continued to talk about how difficult it would be to find an audience for the piece. This gave me a clue about her obstacle. I tested my idea by interrupting and asking her a question:

Rebecca: *So that's my moral tale. And, um (shrugs, then holds hand over mouth) I don't really know who to tell it to. So, uh (holds hand over mouth and sighs). Because, the problem with it is, it's not a children's story, and it obviously can't be told to people who object to the lesson or to babies being put afloat without anyone to ....*

Coach: *I'm going to stop you, Rebecca. What are you doing right now?*

Rebecca: *Judging the limitations of the story. Or of the idea.*

Coach: *Why are you doing that?*

Rebecca: *Because I'm afraid that my ideas can't be accepted, because they don't fit into a category.*

Coach: *So, just in case we might not accept your ideas, you're going to tell us how bad they are?*

Rebecca: *No, I just think people will throw me out, and they won't want me!*

In this exchange, Rebecca told me what her obstacle was. She was feeling afraid that neither she nor her ideas would be accepted. To know how to help her, though, I needed more information about the exact content of the intruding emotional messages. So I asked her to tell part of her story again:

Rebecca: *(Gathers herself, sighs). Well, the one who had been hiding after all the others ran away looked out of the cellar window and saw these strange ships arriving. She heard the terrible cries. On the wind, she could smell the terrible smell. And somehow she found herself thinking of her oldest daughter, the one who had been so good, caring for the babies—until the daughter had declared herself fed up with this work. She had said she was sick of the diapers and the lifting and setting down of wailing babies like she was the sea lifting and setting down the tides. If she ever heard one more baby howl, she had said, she would turn into a monster and haunt the village forever. But ... (laughs, shrugs). I'm sorry.*

At the moment that Rebecca laughed, she made a little shrugging gesture with her hands and neck that seemed to say, "I don't know, don't look at me." I interrupted her:

Coach: *What happened there? You were doing great. And what just happened in the last five seconds?*

Rebecca: *Well, I had a fear that I was interjecting something new and I wasn't sure if it connected. And then I said I'm sorry. But what I was sorry for was ... I wasn't following it myself!*

This telling was more precise and well-worded than the first telling—until she got distracted again. Apparently, Rebecca was fighting an obstacle that came in waves. She would begin to tell her story well. After a little while, though, her fear would crest and take her attention off the story for a moment. She would respond nonverbally, by giggling and giving her shrugging gesture. Or she would suddenly feel lost and say, "I'm sorry." Then she would go back into the story for a while, until the fear crested again.

I began interrupting her whenever she responded to her fear, hoping to make her aware of her feelings and her nonverbal response to them. Each time that I asked what had just happened, there was a slightly different circumstance that had brought her fear to the surface. But each time, she was able to tell more of her story without interrupting it with apologies.

Up to now, I had helped her notice the problem: she would feel fear, and respond to it with distracting mannerisms. But I had neither helped her heal the fear nor given her a positive focus to replace it.

I tried to summarize what was happening:

Coach: *The little giggles are a sign that you're out of the story. Giggles are not necessarily bad, but it looks like, for you, they are a sign that you've "left."*

Rebecca: *I think it's a defense. Yeah.*

Coach: *So get people to listen to you, and ask them to stop you if they see that happening. And just enjoy the story.*

Rebecca: *OK. Yeah. Cause I'm sure that something more might come to me.*

Coach: *Of course! It's just a baby. It's just growing.*

Rebecca: *(Laughs) Oh, my story's a baby! Well, then, I guess it's appropriate!*

In the course of trying to explain, I had stumbled on an image that Rebecca could keep in mind as she tells. The image was waiting in the story: to think of the story as a baby—not an invader—who should be nurtured and treated with love. To turn the image another way, she could also think of herself and the audience as babies, to be treated in the same nurturing, loving way. When telling a story to an audience of babies, she could remind herself, there is nothing to fear.

In this session, there was not time to test the effectiveness of this image for Rebecca. If my hypothesis about it is correct, though, the image will help her conquer the waves of fear. Whatever old experiences left her sometimes afraid of not being accepted, remembering this image will help her notice that those experiences are not repeating in the present. The image will help her reframe the perceived dangerous environment into a nurturing one, and help her respond on the basis of her current situation. When thinking of all of us "babies," therefore, she will not be inhibited by the waves of fear. This will enable her to tell at her best—which will, in turn, increase her likelihood of being well received.

Rebecca's corrective image came from her story. This is most likely not a coincidence. Often, we are drawn to exactly those stories whose images have healing potential for us.

Your most effective image may not come from your story (or other presentation), however. For example, I have a tendency to "reach out and grab" my audience. I may lean forward, I may stand on the edge of the stage, or I may otherwise push myself toward my listeners. This behavior seems related to an emotional block: I feel, unconsciously and chronically, that I have not done enough to reach them. I have found an image, however, that allows me to remember that, in the current situation, I do not need to apply endless effort. I imagine I am sitting cross-legged on top of a ten-foot waterspout. If I lean in any direction, I fall off. But if I am quiescent and confident, the gentle force of the water holds me up. When I tell with this image in mind, I can invite my audience into my story, not push myself toward them.

FIND A STATEMENT OF THE TRUTH

Just as various people need information to be given them in various forms, people need various forms of reminders of the current reality.

Corrective images are especially effective for the storyteller, for two reasons. First of all, the more emotional parts of the human mind seem to prefer the language of imagery. Dreams, art, and the transformation tales of great religions all confirm that imagery may speak louder than discourse, at least where deep feelings are concerned. Second, people who choose to be storytellers are self-selected lovers of imagery.

As powerful as images can be, however, there are times when an equivalent declarative statement of the current truth is more effective. For Rebecca or Brad, such a statement might be something like, "I am safe here, and can expect to be received with love." For Gail, it might be, "Through the power of my love and my joy, this story will help restore women to their full status." In fact, you may find an image more powerful at one time, and at another time you may prefer an equivalent declarative statement.

You may also prefer an image for one kind of emotional block, and a statement for another. As a storyteller, for example, I prefer the imagery of the waterspout to remind me not to push myself at my audience. But I have another block for which I prefer a statement. Normally I find it easy to remain open to my audience, but if the setup of a performance makes me feel highly unappreciated, I tend to withdraw emotionally in anger. Over time, I have discovered that I can remind myself of the the current reality at these moments with this statement: "The only course of action that makes sense is for me is to be completely open to each person here."

TAKE ACTION

The third tool for reminding yourself of the current reality is to take action. As the saying goes, nothing succeeds like success. In the realm of emotional blocks, nothing establishes the difference between earlier situations and your current situation better than taking successful action.

What sort of action should you take? This depends, of course, on the details of your struggle. If the old hurt was being emotionally isolated, for example, take action that connects you to people. If the old hurt was humiliation in front of a group, find group situations where you can receive well-earned praise.

Neil found himself in the grips of feeling powerless. This obstacle led to several unproductive performance behaviors, which he had worked on in several coaching sessions.

One day, Neil told stories in the indoor meeting room of a summer camp while the counselors met in another room. When the children asked for a ghost story, he said to them, "Oh, for a ghost story it should be darker in here." The children chorused, "Let's pull down the window shades!" This encouraged Neil to interrupt the counselor's meeting and request help pulling down the shades.

To his surprise, Neil found that this simple action of taking charge of his performance environment made him feel less powerless, and made it easier to avoid his unproductive performance habits. His action had reminded him that he was not the powerless boy he once had been.

Neil incorporated this reminder into his performance routine by always being sure to ask beforehand, "What choices do I have about how the room is set up?" When he made a choice—any choice!—and had it carried out, it helped remind him of his present, empowered situation.

As your coach, I can be aware of the helping potential of corrective action. Georgina, for example, had been a quiet participant in a four-day beginning workshop in storytelling. Several times, she expressed her fear of telling a story to the group. At last, everyone had taken a turn to be coached but her. Determinedly, she began to tell.

Georgina's story turned out to be a perfect conclusion to the workshop. A literary fable, it told of an apprentice juggler who had difficulty learning the standard rhythm of juggling used by his troupe. When, in the heat of performance, he began to juggle in his own natural rhythm, the king himself praised the apprentice for his unique and beautiful style.

The workshop members and I gave enthusiastic appreciations of Georgina's performance. When it came time for suggestions, I thought to myself, "What is her obstacle? It is only shyness and lack of confidence in her own style—just like in her story. How could I help her remember her competence?"

Rather than dilute her success by giving suggestions, I said, "I have no suggestions worth giving you. That was beautiful just as it was." By offering no suggestion, I let her unconditionally successful performance serve as a corrective action that could stand in her memory as a reminder of her true abilities. Another day, she might need another response from me. But for now, the most helpful way to respond was to let her notice that she had, indeed, done well.

All Three Methods Work Together

In any one coaching session, I will help you to deal with an emotional block by using one or perhaps two of these three approaches. But in the long term, to let the feelings in, to heal the hurt, and to remember the current reality are complementary and mutually reinforcing processes.

If you let in some blocked feelings, you still may need to deal with them later. This is because most emotions that you would habitually block stem from unhealed hurts. Once you pay attention to the unhealed feelings, it establishes that the hurtful situation is past, that you are no longer in distress. This, in turn, signals to the emotional hurt that it will no longer endanger your survival if it heals.

Feelings that are ready to heal demand your attention, almost like a splinter that is ready to emerge from a partially healed wound. Paying attention to your blocked feelings, then, may lead you to feel them more strongly or more often, as they seek to heal once and for all.

Suppose that you let yourself notice feelings of fear of failure. At this point, it may seem that your formerly blocked fear begins to "bother you more." You may then need to find a way, or several ways, to remind yourself more strongly of your current reality. You may choose to find an image, for example, to remind you that you are competent, or that you are no longer expected to succeed at the task you once failed at, or that failure will not have the consequences you most fear.

This will not be the end of the matter, either. By making it clear that you no longer need to fear failure, you also make it clear that, since the emotionally hurtful period is over, there is no need to postpone healing the hurt. You may find yourself more ready to heal the fear by shaking, laughing, or crying.

As you heal the fear of failure, you will gain even more awareness of it and of related hurts, leading perhaps to another cycle of "let the feelings in—remember the current reality—heal—let more of the feelings in."

You may begin to notice that what seemed like failure is more complex or more helpful than you once thought; you will then understand more clearly how your present circumstances differ from your old ones. Or you may find yourself spontaneously creating images or other reminders of your current reality.

Until an emotional hurt is completely healed, you will continue to alternate among letting more of your feelings in, healing your hurt, and remembering your current reality. Your emotional block will hinder you ever less, in ever fewer areas of your endeavors.

Once an emotional hurt is completely healed, however, it will have no more power over you at all. You will be able to imagine the relevant emotion freely, to tell stories about it (or express it in any form) with great emotional power, and to stop feeling it when your story (or job or relationship) requires another feeling. You will have completely overcome this obstacle.

Should I Deal with Feelings at All?

You might be uncomfortable with the whole idea that feelings are a proper subject for coaching. If so, let me remind you of the first ground rule: you are in charge. If you don't want to deal with feelings, don't.

As a coach, I am in a similar situation. If I am uncomfortable dealing with your feelings, I should not. In the words of psychotherapist Bob Poole, "I should only do what I'm 'up for.' " Pretending to be comfortable with feelings only adds confusion and mistrust.

Declining to work with your feelings, however, is different from being blind to them. I still have an obligation to help you discover your obstacle.

Imagine that I'm a roofer. You bring me to your house to look at a wet ceiling, which, unbeknownst to you, is caused by a leak in a nearby pipe. It's perfectly appropriate for me to say, "I think you need the help of a plumber." On the other hand, it is inappropriate and harmful for me to pretend that plumbing problems don't exist. I must not give your house treatment for a roof leak, just because I don't fix pipes.

In the same way, I must be alert to the possibility that your obstacle is an emotional block, even if I am unwilling or unable to help you with it. I can say, "It looks like you need help with the feelings here, and I'm not comfortable trying to give it. Perhaps I can help you think of who could help." This is helpful.

Having identified your emotional obstacle, I can also offer to help you with other obstacles you may face.

But I must not treat your emotional block as though it is a lack of information, a need for more experience of the story, or misdirected effort. If I do, I will only compound your obstacle by adding extraneous information, confusion, or misconceptions.

THE CASE FOR FORGING AHEAD

Throughout most of human history, emotions have been considered to be part of daily life. They belonged at the hearth side as well as in artistic and religious experiences and relationships.

We are arguably the first culture to take the expression of strong feelings out of the realm of ordinary life and put it into the realm of specialists. Especially in the middle and wealthy classes, we tend to be afraid of feelings. If someone starts to cry, we often think, "Oh, no! I don't know what to do," or "Don't do that! You might start something that will never stop!"

In many ways, helping you with your feelings is like coaching you in other areas. For starters, I keep in mind the same basic principles. I believe in your success—that you can prevail over any internal difficulties. I give praise, focusing on your many strengths even as I witness where you have difficulty. I keep you in charge of the goals. I try to increase your emotional safety.

I can even use the coaching structure for helping you with any feelings. Most importantly, I begin by listening.

If you wish, I can also offer you appreciations, saying something like, "Would you like to hear what I respect in you through all this?"

If you wish—and here it is especially important to suppress our cultural habit for giving advice—I can offer you any suggestions I might have. "Suggestions" can take the form of the techniques outlined in this chapter: helping you notice your feelings, helping you go through the natural healing process for emotional hurts, and helping you remember the current reality.

Finally, I can ask you if you want anything else from me.

My choice is not between knowing everything about feelings and shunning them. If I am willing to help in the way I can, I can leave you to get from others the rest of the help you need.

If I am willing to simply listen to you well, I can be helpful to you. As in all coaching, most of your potential benefit comes from this one simple step of mine. In the case of emotions, furthermore, my listening can also reach directly to the root of your obstacle—as you share your hurt and notice through my compassionate presence itself that you are not at this moment powerless, alone, or in danger.

Finding the Key Obstacle

To help you succeed when you are faced with an obstacle, I need to be familiar with each of the four kinds of obstacles, and with ways to help you overcome them.

At any one moment, however, you will in all likelihood face more than one obstacle. Therefore, I need an additional skill: the ability to decide what help to give when I have many choices.

When faced with multiple obstacles, I think of loggers in the north woods. Before the days of logging trucks, they sent felled trees to the saw mill by floating them down a river. Inevitably, at some point a log would get stuck on a rock or sunken tree. Other logs, in turn, would get stuck on the first log. In time, enough logs could accumulate to block the entire river.

Faced with such a log jam, the loggers sought an effective strategy for restoring the flow. It was hopeless to start with the last logs to get stuck; the loggers might have to remove thousands of logs individually. They discovered, however, that if they could find the first log to get stuck, removing it might allow all the other logs to flow. Therefore, they devoted their efforts to finding and removing the key log.

In the same way, I will help you most effectively if I can identify and help you overcome your key obstacle.

Avoiding the Sham Obstacle

Many times, the first obstacle to appear will only be a veil over the fundamental obstacle. Mending the veil will not help you succeed.

Because the need for information is the only obstacle that is widely acknowledged in our society, people often present their obstacle as a request for information when, in fact, they face an obstacle of a different sort.

Barbara began her coaching session this way:

Barbara: *I don't want to tell you a story. I want to spend my time having you instruct me in vocal technique. My voice gets husky and tired after only one performance.*

Often, your coaching time will be better spent in thinking aloud or in getting questions answered than in telling a long story. In this case, however, I needed clues about how Barbara was misusing her voice. Therefore, I asked her to tell three minutes of a story.

Barbara told her story with verve and humor. But the striking thing about Barbara's vocal technique was her breathless rushing from one phrase to the next. As I listened more intently, I noticed that she didn't seem to give herself enough time to inhale. Since I tend to breathe along with the storyteller, I found myself getting dizzy for lack of breath!

Anyone's voice would get tired from trying to speak loudly without taking in more than a tiny breath. We naturally tend to stop and breathe when we are breathless—unless there is misdirected effort.

WHAT CAUSED HER NOT TO BREATHE?

The question now was, why did Barbara deprive herself of time to breathe, and how could I help her stop? My first thought was to help her become aware of what she was doing.

Coach: *You do something unusual with your breathing.*
Barbara: *A lot of people have told me that.*

Clearly, I wasn't the first to call her attention to her breathing! But there must be some way I could help her experience her own effort.

Coach: *Are you willing to try an exercise right now?*

Barbara: *Sure, I'm desperate.*

Coach: *I want you to tell a little bit of that same story. But every time you breathe in, I want you to breathe twice. Take one whole breath in, then let it out completely. Then breathe in again and continue speaking.*

I stood beside Barbara as she tried this exercise. She took the extra breath at the end of a section of her story, but took many small, hurried breaths in between. Evidently, she wasn't aware enough of her breathing to make use of this exercise.

I tried saying, "Now!" whenever she took a breath—but this made her turn to face me each time I spoke and seemed to make her forget her story.

Next, I stood behind the audience:

Coach: *I'm going to "conduct" your breathing. I'll hold my arms out to my sides and raise them up when it's time for you to breathe in. When they go down, you breathe out. Are you ready and willing?*

Barbara: *I'll try.*

After a minute or two of me "conducting" her breathing, Barbara succeeded in doing the exercise for three or four breaths in a row. At this point, her face looked as though she felt very uncomfortable.

Coach: *How does that feel?*

Barbara: *It feels weird.*

This was progress! Perhaps the "weirdness" Barbara was feeling was caused by not misdirecting her effort in her accustomed way.

Coach: *Tell me more.*

Barbara: *It feels like I'm taking too long.*

Coach: *What would happen if you took too long?*

Barbara: *You wouldn't listen to me anymore.*

At this point, Barbara looked a little embarrassed. Then her eyes shifted up and to the side as though she was remembering something. I suspected that she had more to say, so I just looked at her approvingly and waited. In a few seconds, she spoke:

Barbara: *You see, I had an older sister. We got along fine, but at the dinner table she would always interrupt me. I never got to finish what I was saying.*

This was clearly the source of her misdirected effort: she was trying to prevent us from interrupting her, by not pausing to breathe.

Giving a New Focus

After Barbara spoke a little more about her childhood experiences, I tried giving her a new place to direct her effort.

Coach: *Look around you. Is there anyone here who is trying to speak or to interrupt you?*

Barbara: *They look pretty interested.*

Coach: *Your job is to remember that you have the floor. For the duration of your story, we are not only interested in hearing you, we want you to succeed. We want to hear the whole story. Every audience wants that—at least deep down. If they forget, you can remind them.*

At this point, Barbara looked glowing. She was smiling with apparent pleasure, and standing straighter than before.

Barbara: *I've been to so many voice teachers! They told me to do this and do that with my diaphragm, but I never felt I got what they were saying.*

Coach: *I think you've got it. Want to try telling the same part again, keeping in mind that we want you to tell it all?*

Her new telling was vastly improved.

Barbara's request for information was only a veil over her actual obstacle, misdirected effort. Because I believed in her success, I knew she must be corrupting her own breathing for a reason. This led me to search for and find her misdirected effort.

Was Barbara's obstacle really an emotional block? Barbara's misdirected effort was an attempt to prevent a feeling; this obstacle closely resembles one kind of emotional block. The difference between them is only a matter of degree. When the feeling you are trying to avoid is relatively accessible and your effort is proportionately more significant, I think of your obstacle as misdirected effort. When the feeling is strongly blocked or bigger in significance to you, or when the effort to avoid it is small or absent, however, I think of your obstacle as an emotional block.

It's not important for me to "diagnose" the exact obstacle, especially when it is on the border between two categories. What matters is that I'm aware of the different kind of help that may be needed. Barbara responded well to redirecting her effort. If she hadn't, I would have gone on to try helping her with blocked emotion.

Recognizing the Key Obstacle When I Find It

Many obstacles can be present at once. I need to be able to peel away any surface obstacles and to help you with your key obstacle. Sometimes, I will help you overcome an obstacle, only to find another beneath it.

How can I know when I have found the essential obstacle? Just like the loggers searching for the key log in a jam, I know because—once I have removed the obstacle—the flow is restored to the river.

THE CLEVER MAN AND THE SIMPLE MAN

Steve began his session by telling a long, mystical Jewish story about two friends, a clever man and a simple man. They grew up together, then separated. The clever man, apprenticed to a traveling merchant, learned to sell as well as his master could. Not satisfied, he mastered in turn the worlds of business, goldsmithing, jewelry, and medicine.

The other major character in Steve's story was the simple man, who stayed at home and remained poor. Here's how Steve described the simple man:

Steve: *Each night he would come home and say, "I'd like some kasha, some broth, some beef." And his wife would give him a crust of bread, but he would chew it as if it were manna from heaven. And when he went out, he would ask for his fur coat. And his wife would hand him the old pelt that they shared between the two of them, but he would wear it with pride.*

Steve told his story confidently, but something about it was not effective. If pressed, I would have said that the disturbing quality lay in his tone of voice—but there was no obvious flaw to pinpoint.

So how could I proceed? The only hope was to get more information about whatever obstacle Steve faced.

NEEDING MORE EXPERIENCE

Fortunately, others at the workshop asked Steve some questions. Tony asked Steve why the simple man felt content with his poverty and with the ridicule of his neighbors. Steve answered, and then Amy responded to his answer:

Steve: *He's at peace with himself, and he feels that they don't have that tranquility, that peace that he does have.*

Amy: *How come? How come he has that? I think that's a good question, Tony.*

Steve: *Because he believes. Knowing it's a Hasidic tale, I think you would have to interpret that he has faith, that he believes in what he does and where he is. I think I would have to look at it more, but it's a real good question.*

Amy and Tony sensed that Steve was not completely clear about the simple man and his feelings. So they pointed Steve toward more experience of the story.

LACK OF INFORMATION

Was needing more experience of the story an obstacle? I believed it was. Was it the key obstacle? My intuition suggested it was not. Something else was bothering me, something more to do with Steve's approach to the telling of the story.

The clue I seized upon was in Steve's response to Amy's question. Steve said, "Knowing it's a Hasidic story ...." In short, the genre of a story helps determine our reaction to it.

Hearing that, I knew what I was thinking: his way of telling the story was somehow at odds with the genre of the story. Therefore, he might need information about the genre of the story. So I tried giving some information about the Hasidic fairy tale and its requirements compared to other genres of Hasidic stories (such as tales to teach a moral lesson, tales to show the powers of a particular Hasidic master, or tales to reveal the limitations of conventional learning).

Coach: *And this genre has different ways of working than the other kinds of Hasidic stories. The other kinds of stories are actually much more intellectual. This is much more a story of images.*

For that to work, certain things have to happen. We have to be free to go into a trance. And, I think instinctively you did a lot of this. You told it in a very settled way. You know, if you're leading us into a trance, you want us to be able to follow you into deep places. You don't want to be doing a song and dance, because that takes us out of the trance. You want us to be able to settle back.

I went on to tell Steve in a few sentences how the "trance story" makes special demands on the teller. I explained how the teller needs to try to create extra emotional safety for the audience while simultaneously entering an emotionally open state himself—even as the audience becomes more unresponsive, leaving the teller with less and less feedback.

Did gaining this information help Steve overcome his obstacle? To find out, I asked him to tell the story again, with the new information in mind.

When he retold part of the story, it was completely unchanged!

Does this mean that lack of information was not the key obstacle? Perhaps. But it was also possible that the information had not yet been presented in a way that was meaningful for Steve. I had given the information in a conceptual form. Could

Steve make use of the same information if it came in the form of a metaphor? I tried again. I asked Steve to sit down, to focus him physically. Then I gave him an image that described an approach to the story:

Coach: *You don't have to hypnotize us, you just have to tell it very straightforwardly. Imagine this setting. The party's over in the cottage, the dancers and the drummers and the fiddlers have had their time, the hush settles over almost naturally, and this is the moment when the old person next to the fire starts to speak.*

When Steve began to retell his story now, it was transformed! It had an unadorned intensity and a clarity of tone that seemed to invite the listeners into the story.

Clearly, the information was now in a form that could help him overcome an obstacle. For a few moments, I thought that he had overcome his key obstacle and that my job was done for the day.

Misdirected Effort

As Steve continued to tell his story, however, he began slipping back into his old approach. It seemed that the information obstacle had been overcome but that a second obstacle was lurking below the first one. To make sure, I interrupted him when he began to lose his new approach:

Coach: *I'm going to stop you there. It was great until you got to right there. Do you see what you did?*

Steve: *I got powered up.*

Coach: *Yeah, you got powered up. You're feeling like you have to do something, to come out to us. And what you had been doing is much more as though you're in touch with a deep power, and you're inviting us in.*

Steve was now noticing some misdirected effort. For some reason, he was not content to tell the story as simply and directly as the imagined old person next to the cottage fire. He thought he needed to continue to reach out to us, to wrestle our attention into the story—even though we were already in a trancelike state of complete attention.

To help with Steve's misdirected effort, I instructed him to focus on inviting the audience to come to him, rather than on reaching out to "grab" the audience.

Again, I asked him to continue the story—so that I could learn whether I had helped him correct the misconception that caused him to tell too aggressively. By watching his face carefully, I could see that he was still struggling with his approach to the story. So I interrupted him again:

Coach: *OK, you're doing good. But there's something leading you astray, and you keep noticing it and pulling back, right? [Steve nods]. What's leading you off?*

Steve: *I don't know. It's not my style to be that laid-back, I guess. Although ... Maybe that's what it is. I'm afraid that I'm just telling a story ...*

Coach: *Oh, no, not that!*

Steve: *[laughs] Yeah, yeah. Cause sometimes I'm told—somebody once said to me, "It sounds like a story you're telling me, instead of being a storyteller." And maybe for this story what I need to do is just tell a story.*

Coach: *I can tell you that if you want trance, the thing you were doing when you weren't getting self-conscious and saying, "Oh, my God, I've got to make it exciting," was much more effective.*

Steve: *Good. And that's just doing it, and convincing myself and then hearing it back on tape or something.*

Coach: *In general, trance stories are very hard, from the point of view that you don't get a lot back from the audience—because we're busy doing this [drops jaw]. We're deep. We're gone.*

Steve: *Yeah. And I guess that's really the best response.*

At this point, it seemed clear that Steve's continuing misdirected effort was caused by an emotional block.

EMOTIONAL BLOCK

Even though Steve now understood that his goal in this story was to enable his listeners to settle back into a trancelike state, he was still afraid that it wouldn't be good enough unless he put effort into making the story "interesting." His fear was blocking his ability to put his understanding into practice.

I stated my conclusion back to Steve and waited to hear his response—to make sure he didn't have any corrections for me.

Coach: *So, it sounds like the thing that pulls you off is just your fear that you're boring.*

Steve: *Yeah, I think maybe you're right. And I think it's just a matter of having the confidence that I know what I'm doing, and working it through, doing it.*

Coach: *And the tricky thing about a trance story is that you won't get the feedback until the story's over.*

I had one more goal: I wanted to leave Steve with a reminder of his current reality. As I was talking to him, it occurred to me that the story contained a corrective image:

Coach: *So, talk about leaps of faith! You've chosen a great story to help your development as a storyteller.*

Steve: *[laughs]. True, true, true.*

Coach: *And part of what you need to learn, just like in the story, is that the simple, satisfied way ....*

Steve: *Good point, good point. Learn from my own story.*

Coach: *Learn from your own story. And in fact, the story can remind you. "Oh! Tell it like the simple man would tell it, not the way the clever one would."*

Steve: *Yeah. I mean, the simple man was the teacher of the story.*

To help him overcome the essential, emotional obstacle, my job was to notice each obscuring obstacle and help him overcome it. When I helped with one obstacle, another one would come to the surface and take its place—until, finally, the underlying fear could be revealed and addressed. At this point, Steve was finally ready to go back and experience the story more. With the emotional block neutralized, he could now allow his imagination to explore the feelings and world view of the simple man.

Without his emotionally driven search for reassurance, he would not misapply effort, which in turn would leave him free to explore the genre and gain more experience of the story's meanings.

TWO WAYS TO RECOGNIZE SUCCESS

In Steve's session, I encountered an obstacle, then tried to help him overcome it. To know if I had actually helped him, I asked him to try telling the story again. I judged my success by his success.

When he told with the same symptoms, I usually concluded that I had not yet helped him with the obstacle. When the symptoms changed, however slightly, I usually concluded that Steve had encountered a new obstacle. Thus, each retelling gave me valuable information.

The clearest indication that I have helped you overcome your key obstacle is that you are now succeeding where before you did not. Having you retell your story can allow me to see you succeed. In a group setting, I can judge by the reactions of the other listeners as well as by my own reaction.

Sometimes, however, it is not possible to witness success within a single coaching session. Some obstacles take longer than one session to be overcome. Sometimes you will just need to rest before applying what you have learned.

In these cases, I can rely on another indicator of success. If the flow has been restored, you will appear energized. Like Barbara, you may "glow." You may seem more like your true self. You will seem excited, involved, empowered. Whether joyfully or solemnly, you will be enthusiastic about continuing your progress toward success.

Flexible Persistence

It is not important that I identify your key obstacle immediately. But it is important that I *try* to identify it, and that I make efforts to help you. Then I must notice their results, and change my efforts based on your response.

I can't be infallible. But I can persist flexibly.

I can't solve every problem. But I can get help when I'm stuck.

FAILING CHEERFULLY

When introducing herself to the other members of a weekend workshop, Carla made it clear that she didn't think of herself as a storyteller. A kindergarten teacher for thirty years, she rarely told stories even to her students. At story swaps, others begged her to tell, but she had no idea why they wanted to hear her.

When it was Carla's turn to be coached, she prefaced her story with another remark about, "I probably shouldn't be here. You can give someone else my time."

At my insistence, Carla took her turn to be coached. In her session, she chose to tell a story.

It was magnificent. Her telling had simplicity and delight.

When it was time for appreciations, the workshop members tried to convince Carla how much they had loved her story. Carla listened politely, but almost seemed intent on not believing them.

When it was time for suggestions, I said:

Coach: *You don't need to learn how to tell stories. You need to tell them more! Why don't you?*

Carla: *I guess I don't think I do it that well.*

Clearly, Carla's main obstacle was her lack of self-esteem as a storyteller, because it prevented her from telling more and thus gaining further experience. My job was somehow to help her see the value of her telling. I tried getting her to notice how much we had all loved her story.

Carla: *Well, these are my friends from story-sharing group. Of course they'd say that.*

After a few more tries along the same lines, it became clear that Carla's opinion of her telling was so low that she interpreted praise as insincere. There must be some emotional block that kept her from changing her hard-line opinion about her telling, even in the face of substantial contrary evidence.

I tried several ways to make her aware of her feelings. I asked her about experiences in her life that left her feeling incompetent. She told matter-of-factly how she had felt like a failure for her first years as a kindergarten teacher. But she experienced no feelings attached to those memories, she said.

Next, I tried several ways to give her a chance to heal whatever emotional hurt might be keeping her from noticing how well she told. Some of my attempts seemed to confuse her. Others clearly repelled her.

Next, I attempted to find a reminder of her current reality as a competent adult. I tried at least a half-dozen approaches. Nothing worked!

GETTING HELP FOR MYSELF

At this point, we had spent thirty minutes. Carla had about ten minutes left to her coaching session. All I had really learned was the nature of her obstacle and about twenty approaches to overcoming it that didn't work.

I was stuck.

It never comes easily to me to admit that I'm stuck. But over the years I have learned the wisdom of doing so. I swallowed my false pride and said to the group:

Coach: *I'm stuck. I'd like to stop Carla's session for five minutes, and ask those of you who are willing to listen to me think aloud for five minutes.*

Carla agreed to interrupt her session and let me talk about it. The group agreed to listen to me.

During my five minutes, I summarized what I had learned about Carla's obstacle, and the main approaches I had tried that had failed.

At this point, one of the workshop participants said, "Can I make a suggestion you could try? Ask her to remember the faces of her children when she tells them stories."

This was a wonderful suggestion, but it was close to one I

had tried. I thought that Carla would diminish the value of her students' response in some way.

Coach: *Nothing that she hears from her audience is going to convince her that she can tell well. The only thing she has ever really accepted doing well is her teaching.*

Even as I rejected the suggestion, this exchange made me think of one more thing to try. I ended my five minutes. Then, with Carla's permission, I returned to her session:

Coach: *Carla, do you believe that you teach kindergarten well?*

Carla: *Now I do.*

Coach: *If I were an angel perching on your shoulder thirty years ago, saying "Keep teaching; one day you'll see that you're good at it," would you believe me?*

Carla: *Yes, I can see that.*

Coach: *Would you be glad that you listened?*

Carla: *Yes.*

Coach: *Well, I'd like you to imagine that I am that same angel come back. Only this time I say, "Keep telling stories; one day you'll see that you're good at it." Can you imagine saying in thirty years, "I'm glad that I listened"?*

Carla: *Yes. I see what you mean. I have to trust.*

Coach: *Your students will thank you for taking the risk to trust that angel. Everyone who hears your stories will thank you.*

Carla: *I think I get it.*

Coach: *Can we spend the rest of your time figuring out how to work more storytelling into your life?*

Carla: *OK.*

At last, I had found—a reminder of the current reality—the image of the angel whom she is willing to believe—that worked for Carla.

What I Did Well

I succeeded in helping Carla overcome her obstacle because I did three things.

First, I identified her obstacle. In this case, that was the easy part! Nonetheless, it is the foundation of all further progress.

Second, I succeeded in maintaining flexible persistence. As soon as it was clear that one approach was not working, I cheerfully went on to try another one.

Third, I got help for myself when I was stuck. This began with admitting that I was stuck. For me, that admission is often difficult. Then I asked for help and made use of it.

At the end of the weekend workshop, the participants gave me appreciations for coaching. Carla's was, "Thanks for not giving up on me."

When to Stop Trying

My persistence is a great tool in helping to overcome your obstacle.

But, like any tool, it can do harm if applied rigidly.

Flexibility consists of changing my efforts based on your response. Sometimes, flexibility means knowing when to stop for the day.

It's always difficult for me not to reach the point where you have overcome your obstacle. But sometimes, it's enough to simply identify your obstacle.

NEEDING INFORMATION ABOUT TANDEM TELLING?

Two eighth-graders, Olivia and Jennifer, were telling a folktale in tandem. In their story, Jennifer portrayed a harried farmer whose house seems too noisy. Olivia portrayed the rabbi who instructs the farmer to bring more and more animals into the house. When the farmer has all his animals inside and things are noisier than ever, the rabbi instructs the farmer to remove all the animals at once. Now, the farmer's house seems quietly peaceful.

When their classmates made suggestions, one mentioned that she wasn't always sure what Jennifer had been portraying.

Jennifer used effective mime in her portrayal of the farmer.

Yet she used few spoken words. As a result, her audience was often unsure exactly what the farmer was doing or how he felt about it.

Often, tandem storytellers start to act out a scene and then forget that they can return to the role of narrators. Thinking that Jennifer might need information about her narrative options, with her permission I explained her choices to her:

Coach: *You have a bunch of choices. You can keep acting it out silently, like what you just did. When you do this, you have to show us your character's reaction as well as his tasks.*

Or you can talk as the character as you do it. [Demonstrates.] "Oh, I can't believe I'm supposed to bring in a cow .... It's already so noisy. Listen to that! This place is worse than it was!" That's another choice.

And the third choice is to be the narrator. You can tell the story as you do what the farmer does. [Demonstrates.] "And so the farmer pushed the cow in. But the cow began to moo. It didn't make things quieter at all."

Do you see what I mean? You have all those choices. Is there one that seems good to you?

Jennifer chose the second choice, to speak in the farmer's voice as she acted out his actions. But when she tried to redo the scene, she did not add his words.

Coach: *Did you forget to let him speak? This time, let's figure out beforehand some of what you're going to say, so you don't have to think of it when you're doing it.*

Jennifer worked out three lines to say. Then she got ready to say them while acting out what her character did. As she began, she started to giggle, then stopped her story.

Coach: *Keep going! You're doing good. It's embarrassing, but you're doing good.*

Jennifer: *You know, this house isn't getting any smaller! [Giggles.]*

At this moment, I glimpsed Jennifer's likely obstacle. She was very comfortable being expressive through movements, but much less comfortable using her voice expressively. Her obstacle was not lack of information, but an emotional block. She was embarrassed to use her voice to show the character's feelings.

To help her overcome her obstacle, I would probably want to help her heal some of her embarrassment, as I had done with Brad ("Try Out Being Afraid," page 163.) But the mood in the classroom at the moment did not seem right for working on embarrassment. Compared to the classroom session in which I coached Brad, the group looked more impatient. Jennifer, too, looked less eager to take on her obstacle. After all, she had already endured a long (potentially embarrassing)turn in the coaching spotlight.

As much as I wanted to help Jennifer overcome her obstacle right then, I judged that my efforts were likely to fail unless I waited for another day. I had to settle for a hypothesis about her obstacle, to which I could return.

To end on a positive note, I appreciated what Jennifer had just done:

Coach: *That was good! Did you see how her body language showed us how she felt about bringing in the cow? Jennifer, you can try it a bunch of different ways, if you like. That was very effective, though, to me, what you just did.*

PRIORITIZE

As your coach, I notice as many of your obstacles and symptoms of obstacles as I can. Then I decide which obstacle seems to be fundamental. I give highest priority to assisting you with this key obstacle. If time remains, I can assist you with other obstacles as well.

One mechanical aid to this prioritization process is for me to take notes as you tell your story or make your presentation. Some excellent coaches prefer not to take notes, but I find that it helps me. After your story, I can read through all the possible obstacles that I noted, asking myself about each one, "Is this the key obstacle?" Frequently, this review helps me identify a general obstacle that wasn't apparent at any single moment in the story.

I must also prioritize in another way.

The more experience I gain as a coach, the more I can look at you now and see the storyteller you can become. Sometimes I can see several steps ahead of your current development.

Naturally, it is tempting for me to help you take two, three, or four steps all at once. Equally naturally, giving in to this temptation usually confuses, overwhelms or discourages you.

Therefore, I must also prioritize in sequence. What step are you ready to take now? Of two or three possible steps, which one actually makes the most sense to do first?

✧ A LIFETIME SUPPLY ✧

Fresh out of school, a new M.B.A. got a very high position in an overseas company—in a country about which he knew nothing.

In a panic, he went to a retired consultant who had made his fortune in that very country.

"I leave in two weeks for my new career! I may never see you again. Before I go, you must tell me everything you learned about doing business in that land."

The consultant said, "I understand your urgency. But let me ask you one thing. Think of all the bread you will eat in the years you are there—several tons of it. Would it really help you if I gave you all that bread at once?"

YET ANOTHER BALANCE

Personally, I find it easier to persist as a coach, and harder to wait patiently for another day. When I leave you discouraged or dissatisfied, it is usually because I tried to accomplish too much in the time available. Other coaches, I am sure, have more relaxed confidence about your future, and more difficulty in persisting today.

At the same time that I try to keep a balance between your needs and mine, between your needs and the needs of a group, between appreciation and suggestions, between healing past hurts and remembering the current reality—I must also keep a balance between persistence and patience.

Coaching in the Classroom

Coaching is a powerful method for helping people learn efficiently and eagerly. When you learn to coach, you become a more effective helper.

To put coaching into practice, you need to understand coaching in general and then adapt coaching to your own setting.

The previous chapters of this book helped you understand what coaching is. The first chapter of this book described the principles of coaching: believing in the student's success, honoring the student's goals, giving praise, and creating safety.

The second chapter gave a four-part structure that can be used to incorporate those principles in a wide variety of situations: listening, giving appreciations, giving suggestions, and asking what else the student wants.

The next chapters helped you recognize and give assistance with the common obstacles to success. The examples were taken from my experiences coaching storytellers in private sessions and in workshops. In these settings, coaching is a self-contained activity, removed from the flow of daily life.

The current chapter is about adapting coaching to the classroom. Starting with the coaching of storytelling, it flows into the coaching of all subjects of the curriculum. This chapter helps you integrate coaching into other activities, to make them go better with less intervention from you—ultimately to make your job easier and more enjoyable.

COACHING TO THE RESCUE

Once, as part of a program on recognizing diversity, I taught seventh-graders to collect life stories from elders in their communities. They returned to their classrooms to tell their favorite episodes from the stories they had learned.

One student told his entire class the story he had collected from an older man. The student had memorized the story dutifully, and told it with an eye on the teacher's reaction. The teacher looked hopeful, then distressed at the student's increasingly confused, dreary recitation. Seeing her expression, the student floundered. His worry turned to panic. His story lost coherence and stuttered to an embarrassed halt.

Many teachers would have known only a few responses to make in this situation, such as grading the performance (maybe giving credit for effort), or making a not-too-harsh comment, or telling the student to repeat the story, but to "use more expression and make it more lively!"

Fortunately, this teacher had agreed to learn about coaching. With my help, she elicited comments from the others about what they liked in the story. The student storyteller seemed worried, then relieved, then interested in the effect that the beginning of his story had had.

Now that the student was aware that others found his story worthy of some interest, he seemed ready for help in improving it. I asked him, "What do you love about the story?" He answered, "I think it's cool that he did what he did. It was dangerous."

I asked, "What was the dangerous part?"

"Those other kids could have hurt him, and still he tried to help his friend."

After a few more questions, he was telling his whole story again—but with gusto. He had connected to his own interest in the story, and his interest had animated his voice, his body, and his choice of words. Now his telling was lively and clear.

Not only the student storyteller had succeeded. The rest of us had succeeded, too—as listeners, as coaches. The room came alive with our shared sense of proficiency and purpose. A potentially humiliating experience had turned into an adventure in which we had helped each other become heroes.

This chapter will help you learn to create similar upward spirals of success and interest.

First, it will help you integrate your role as coach with your other roles as teacher. It gives special comments for teachers about topics covered in the rest of this book.

Second, it introduces you to the even greater benefits that come from teaching your students to coach each other. Your student coaches will take some of the burden of teaching from you. And for them, it will not be a burden, but a powerful new tool that will further accelerate their own learning.

The four-part coaching structure is a basic organizing structure for classrooms, equivalent to raising hands before speaking, or to lining up before leaving the room. Once students have learned the structure, they can apply it to any subject—just as students who know how to line up can then go anywhere.

This chapter ends by describing the use of coaching across the curriculum—to energize your students and support their confidence. Coaching can be adapted for subjects that may seem very far from storytelling, including math and science. Once you have taught your students to coach each other in a variety of subjects, your role will begin to change to resemble more what you originally wanted it to be when you became a teacher: not a disciplinarian, but a facilitator of others' learning.

Coaching Principles in the Classroom

Many teachers will immediately accept the principles of coaching. Some have been applying them successfully for years; others have wanted to. Nonetheless, many other teachers will have serious questions about them. What follows are the most common questions, and my responses.

IS THE DIVERSITY OF SUCCESS RELEVANT TO THE CLASSROOM?

The first principle of coaching, "Believe in success," (pages

29-32) depends on my believing in the diversity of success: that everyone can succeed in a unique way. Not everyone can be first in her high school class or score in the ninetieth percentile on a standardized test. Success can be defined individually, however, rather than in terms of comparison and competition.

In the school setting, this might be a big stretch from current school or community operating assumptions. Yet it is both possible and desirable. To believe otherwise is to give up in advance on a percentage of your students. No teacher really wants to abandon any student to failure.

Each student is a unique gift to the universe, with a unique set of abilities and a unique point of view. Your job is to help each student become himself or herself. Nothing less does justice to the student or to you.

Don't We All Need the Same Skills?

"But," you might say, "don't we all need a basic set of skills? Why insist on the diversity of success? (pages 30-32) What's wrong with teaching uniform, basic competencies?"

I'm in favor of basic competencies. I'm glad I learned to read, write, and multiply; these skills have helped me do many things. The problem is not with the skills, but with forgetting why they are important.

Basic skills are important to my student because they help him accomplish what he really wants to accomplish.

In other words, what's "basic" about the basic skills is that they help with many, many goals. If we start from eliciting and honoring our students' goals, the road to success will lead through the basic skills for almost everyone.

The "shortcut" of saying, "These skills will help you; wait and see!" often turns into a tortuous detour. When students need basic skills to achieve their goals, they will learn them quickly and well. Until then, they may at best humor us by studying without passion; at worst, they will resist what they see as oppressive and meaningless.

The actual shortcut to basic skills is to elicit and honor the students' goals, then to help students achieve their goals. If our students learn to perceive us as allies to their goals, they will eventually come begging us to help them learn basic skills. If a student is not eager to learn basic skills, she must need help at some other stage of the process—perhaps in the very skills of goal-setting. Directing our effort at forcing students to learn unsought skills will only further obscure the obstacle they need help to overcome.

HONOR THEIR GOALS? ALL THEY WANT TO DO IS GOOF OFF!

Honoring students' goals (pages 32-35) can be a challenge for teachers, who have been surrounded by the idea (often unspoken) that children learn only when forced.

If children had no trustworthy inner drive to learn, they would not learn to walk or to speak. They would not spend hours of free time mastering sports, hobbies, or dinosaur names.

The apparent lack of inner motivation so evident in many students is not the cause of our failure to teach them well, but the symptom of our inappropriate methods. The less we connect learning to their goals, the less they learn. The less they learn, the more we try to force them to learn, "because we say so." We create a spiral of disconnection and coercion.

How do *you* respond to school boards, administrators and legislators telling you what you should do? Would you waste your time unless they told you what's important?

Your actual job (preferably with the help and support of your entire community and nation) is to help children reconnect with their inner motivation. In this way, honoring children's goals includes helping children develop and articulate their own goals.

To be sure, many students will have goals that do not seem, at first, to relate closely to the curriculum as you know it. In this case, your job will include making it clear to the student how a professional basketball player, for example, needs to know the math of scoring and statistics, the literacy of reading contracts and writing autobiographies, and the biology of his own anatomy for training and dealing with injuries. If you succeed in establishing these applications of school subjects (perhaps through allowing students to create their own projects), you will tap into the vast energies that students commonly reserve for the after-school hours.

In the short term, of course, given the state of siege that students have come to expect, you may need to place temporary limits on students that eventually won't make sense. In the long term, however, it is possible to elicit and develop each child's true desires—and, by helping the child learn about and pursue those desires, help the child gain confidence, ambition, and skills.

DON'T I HAVE TO TELL THEM WHEN THEY'RE WRONG?

Giving praise (pages 35-39) may seem reasonable to you, but you may also feel an obligation to correct students whenever they are incorrect.

In some measure, you are right. It is certainly not a favor to a student to pretend that two plus two equals five, or that a story is working when it is not.

The important point, however comes when deciding what to do about incorrect or ineffective results.

If pointing out defects always worked, we would have a nation of highly competent scholars.

All too often, negative comments focus the student's attention on what *not* to do. This keeps the student thinking about not swallowing her words, about not saying "uh," or about not forgetting the third export product of Senegal. This brings the student further from her desires to understand and communicate, which are the wellsprings of her success. When this happens, negative comments can lead to new kinds of failure.

Most often, the quickest way to improvement leads not through criticism, but through noticing and appreciating what the student is doing well already. Then you can notice where the obstacle is, and give the appropriate help.

Further, responding only to the wrongness of an answer can

be dehumanizing. "Objective scoring," with its appealing aura of certainty and simplicity, can be an excuse for not treating the learner as a person with an internal learning process—in short, for objectifying not just the answer but also the student.

BUT MY STUDENTS ARE NOT IN CHARGE!

You are right; your students are not completely in charge ("You are in charge," page 42). Compulsory schooling means that your students are not actually free to leave, or perhaps not even to decide what school to attend or what course of study they enroll in.

You have two conflicting roles. First, you are something like a prison guard, who must keep the inmates from leaving and from hurting each other. Second, you are a teacher, a coach, a facilitator of learning.

You can be frank about these two roles and your interpretation of the boundaries between them. You can make a statement something like the following (amending it to express the degree of choice you are actually willing to extend to your students):

"I am required by law to keep you here, to keep you safe, and to keep you from hurting others. In this regard, I am not just your coach. Within those constraints, though, I hope to coach you and give you freedom of choice."

SAFETY? I DON'T FEEL SAFE HERE MYSELF!

Contemporary teachers face unprecedented dangers within the school itself. In some cases, your physical safety may be in danger, not to mention your job or your autonomy in the classroom.

It is understandable, therefore, that you might feel helpless about making your students feel safe. But you have the unquestionable ability to create certain elements of emotional safety (pages 40-42) for your students. If you fail to maximize their emotional safety to the best of your ability, you undermine your other efforts at helping students learn.

If nothing else, you can avoid making public criticism of students. This form of humiliation is completely in your power to stop.

Next, you can shun criticism of any kind that attacks a student's goodness, intentions, or underlying abilities. Never state or concur that any student is bad, lazy, stupid, or hopeless.

In general, you can always prevent any form of attack that might come from you.

Further, it is vitally important that you protect students from verbal attack by each other. When I teach, I try to seem easygoing and tolerant. But if one student insults another, I become fierce. I say,

"There will be no insults in this class. I will not let anyone put you down, and I will not let you put anyone else down, either. That's the only way it can be safe enough to learn. Can you live with that rule?"

My fierceness is important, because it can assure students that I will protect them.

To increase safety further, ask students' permission before making appreciations or suggestions, before interrupting an activity they are doing, or even before asking them questions. Let them know that they will not be thrust into any situation without warning—or, even better, without their consent.

In general, treat students with maximum respect. You might imagine that each one is a visiting dignitary, and treat them accordingly. This will reduce their need to defend themselves and increase their available attention for learning.

But I Cannot Keep Confidentiality!

A promise of confidentiality in the learning situation ("Everything you say is confidential," page 43) helps make it safe for the student to say whatever needs saying. Freed from the fear of having her remarks or concerns repeated outside the classroom, the student can focus more completely on overcoming the obstacles to her success.

At the same time, confidentiality is never absolute. Other confidential relationships also have limits. Priests and lawyers, for examples, face circumstances when they must betray a confidence in order to protect someone from serious harm. The role of teachers is fundamentally similar.

It may make sense to be frank about the limitations on your legal or professional ability to maintain confidentiality. You can explain to your students what circumstances require you to pass on information they share with you. If this provokes discussion, consider having students do research about the limits of confidentiality for reporters, psychotherapists and teachers. Perhaps they will come to understand why things are as they are, or else they may have recommendations for changes in applicable laws or ethical codes.

If you do have an occasion to pass on information that was gathered in confidence, try to be respectful of the student involved. You can say, "Here's what I am going to tell your mother, and why." In an extreme case you can say something like this (in private, of course):

"I promised you that everything you told me would be confidential. But I cannot allow you to continue to be abused. Therefore, I intend to tell the social worker that an anonymous report has been put in, saying .... Do you think this will put you in danger?"

If you take seriously your role as coach, you will need to confront the conflicts with your other roles as guardian and public servant.

The principles of coaching are guidelines for treating people with respect. They make as much sense in school as they do among professional artists or business colleagues.

Notes on the Four-Part Structure

The four-part structure (pages 47-88) is a powerful teaching tool for the classroom.

This section consists of special comments about using the four-part structure to coach your students. A later section, "Students Become Coaches," gives hints about teaching your students to use the four-part structure to coach each other.

LISTENING

Teachers everywhere complain that their students don't listen. At the same time, few teachers seem ready to help their students learn to listen.

By far, the best method to teach listening (pages 48-54) is to listen.

Listen to your students individually. Listen to them in small groups. Listen to individuals who speak to the whole group.

Notice how you listen. Are you quick to interrupt and give corrections? Do you offer suggestions without asking permission? Do you continue another task while a student is speaking to you? If so, you are teaching your students to listen in the same inattentive ways.

Model respectful listening, and guide others to do the same. While listening to a child speak in front of other students, for example, encourage the others to listen as well as you are listening. Gently interrupt any interruptions, saying something like:

"Oops! I don't think Katy was finished with her thought yet."

"Could you tell me that later, when Chi Min has finished?"

Or,

"I'm still listening to Samir."

Besides the habit of inattentive listening, the main reason students don't listen well is that they need to be listened to themselves. Be creative about finding ways to allow your students—especially the ones who interrupt others—to be listened to. Once you have spent a month listening to a "problem listener" for five full minutes three times a week (while walking the child to gym after the others have gone, for example), the child will almost certainly be more able to listen. Further, your refusal to listen at a particular moment will be received in a context of the relative abundance of your attention, not of unrelieved scarcity.

APPRECIATIONS

Young children thrive on appreciations (pages 54-64), and usually accept them enthusiastically.

Older children may feel embarrassed by appreciations. This does not mean you should not give them. Give appreciations at a time when it would not be disruptive for children to express embarrassment (giggling is the most likely form), and in a situation where the appreciations are likely to be accepted (adolescents, for example, may do best when approached alone, out of earshot of peers).

Start by giving the appreciations that are easiest for your students to accept, and work your way gradually to others. In the course of a single school year, even the most resistant group can learn to tolerate—and expect—appreciations of something as personal as their courage or ability to express love, given in front of the group (as long as you do not allude to confidential information in the process).

Incorporate appreciations into your daily classroom schedule. When I taught music to small groups, for example, I ended each session by making contact with each student. One at a time I would shake their hands, thank them for coming to music class, and give them an appreciation.

When I was a preschool teacher, I made the rounds at the beginning and end of each day, giving a private appreciation to each of my sixteen students.

Find unexpected times to appreciate individual children, too. But in all cases, remember to ask permission:

"Can I tell you something I liked about your report?"

"I noticed something wonderful about how you worked with the other students today. Would you like to hear it?"

"Something you did yesterday had a good effect on me. Can I tell you what it was?"

Rephrase these requests in a way that is natural and respectful, given who you and your students are. If your students will respond better to you saying, "Wanna hear a thumbs up?" for example, then ask permission in those words—provided you can do so without pretending or condescending. When in doubt, it is better to speak as you would to another adult whom you respect.

Your tone of voice is always crucial when giving appreciations. With young children, be especially careful not to let other tones of voice (e.g., those used for warnings or for getting the attention of the group) bleed into your appreciations. With older children, be sure to avoid any trace of condescension.

Be thoughtful about stereotypical appreciations. Don't always appreciate a student for the same quality (e.g., one is always pretty, another always smart).

Further, be aware of group stereotypes. Don't appreciate girls only for their looks or compliance, or boys only for their toughness or prowess. To overcome my own unconscious stereotypes, I gave myself occasional "topic days," during which I would appreciate every class member for a particular kind of quality. For example, one day I would appreciate all students individually—boys and girls—for some aspect of their appearance. Another day, I would appreciate all students for something smart they had done that day. I would try to notice my own reactions as I gave these appreciations, thus learning more about my prejudices.

Finally, don't forget to appreciate the entire group and various subgroups. "Today, I really felt you working together. It made me feel good." Or, "The group that was making the poster over in this corner seemed to be respecting each other's thinking. I was impressed!"

SUGGESTIONS

Positive suggestions (pages 66-69) may take effort for you to formulate at first, especially if you are accustomed to making negative suggestions. Yet this effort will pay off a hundred times in increased learning and cooperation. To be sure, some student actors will improve if you make a negative comment like, "Don't just sit there! You look like you're not part of the scene!" But many more students will feel stupid or that you are their adversary. To make them see you as an ally in their learning, translate your thoughts into a positive suggestion: "What does your character care about in this scene? Can you find a way to let your character express that? What if your character actively tried to intervene to get what he wants?"

The key disadvantage of making suggestions (page 47 and pages 65-76) or other comments is triply important in a school setting: suggestions can cause the student to abandon his internal sense of judgment in favor of trying to please the coach.

In a school setting, the power differential between teacher and student is much greater than that between adult storyteller and coach. Our society grants the teacher rights and freedoms unavailable to any child, including the right to come and go at will. Be thoughtful about offering suggestions in this context: any reaction from you can potentially distract your student from his own goals.

This means that you need to be especially careful when you ask a student if she would like to hear a suggestion. Ask clearly. Wait patiently for an authentic response, not just one that implies, "I know you're going to do what you want anyway, so get it over with." Make it doubly clear that the student has a choice.

If you do offer a suggestion, pay attention to the power differential once again. You may need to go to great lengths to make it clear that your suggestions are non-binding. For example, it may make sense to repeat several times in different ways that the student has a choice whether to implement them.

If you also make requirements ("To pass this course, write your story down and turn it in!"), make a clear separation between them and any optional suggestions.

Asking questions (pages 72-76), often the most respectful form of suggestion, has special connotations in the classroom. Classroom questions are often used to demand correct answers rather than to ask about the student's thoughts or desires. In the most extreme form, the classroom question is used to force the student to guess what the teacher is thinking. ("Why is it not nice to mess up my desk, students?") In this context, you will have to be especially careful to indicate that a question is meant to inquire. You may have to surround it with qualifiers, such as "I'm interested to know what you think. There is no right answer. I just thought you might have your own idea about this."

WHAT ELSE WOULD YOU LIKE?

In the classroom setting, where the assumption reigns that the teacher is in charge, you will need to be especially careful to remind the student that he or she is in charge.

Because the question "What else would you like?" (pages 82-83) is almost never asked of students, they may have some difficulty answering it at first. Be patient. It may help to suggest things that a student might want: "I was just wondering if there was any other way we could help you with your story. Is there anything we said that was not clear to you? Was there any part of your story you are still wondering about? Is there anything else you wish we had said?"

Overcoming Obstacles in the Classroom

In general, there is no reason to explain the various types of obstacles (pages 91-176) to children. It makes sense for you as their teacher to be able to name and understand the kinds of obstacles, but most children will do best to respond to them on an unconscious level. Later, when they become interested in how to coach with more awareness, there will be plenty of time to elucidate these advanced concepts.

LACK OF INFORMATION

Because schools so often expect students to master information that has no obvious relevance to the students, be sure to establish the connection between any information you offer and the student's goals.

It may make sense to recapitulate very clearly why you are offering information, and to make extra sure that the student wants the information:

"Let me make sure I understand what help you want. It seems that you would like your story to sound like it really happened in colonial Boston, but you are not sure what the inside of a house there would have looked like. Is that right? So, I could tell you a little about where to find information about colonial houses. Is that what you'd like to have happen right now?"

NEEDING MORE EXPERIENCE OF THE STORY

This is an important obstacle (pages 111-135) for many students, especially because they are often so unaccustomed to being asked about their own interpretations.

The section on questions (pages 130-135) is especially useful for classroom teachers. Respectful questions can be your most important tool in helping students to identify their goals. Only when their goals are identified will your students be likely to throw themselves into work aimed at achieving them.

MISDIRECTED EFFORT

Much misdirected effort in a classroom setting is related to the power imbalance between student and teacher.

In situations where people feel powerless (which includes situations where they are powerless!), they tend to put effort into regaining power or into simple survival.

In the classroom, this means that some students will try to please you, others will defy you, and still others will just try to go along unnoticed.

All three of these forms of effort interfere with learning.

To correct these forms of misdirected effort, you first have to make sure they are not appropriate survival skills. Change your classroom procedures, if necessary, to give your students the maximum freedom of choice appropriate in your situation. The sections later in this chapter on introducing coaching to your students can expedite this process. Make sure that you are following the coaching principles outlined earlier in this book. If only in a single unit of study, give pride of place to the goals of your students.

If your students still misdirect their effort into placating you, defying you, or avoiding your regard, it may help to point out what is happening.

Once I coached a class of high-school seniors. One student (with a reputation as a bright troublemaker) told a story that successfully entertained his classmates. After appreciations, in an attempt to help him make his story even better, I asked him what he liked about the story. His answer rang false to me. When I asked him more about what he liked, I felt I was being stonewalled.

I noticed that I felt angry with him. I asked myself silently, "Why do I feel mad?" The answer came to mind, "He's holding himself back from me." Suddenly, I glimpsed the dynamic between us: he was offering just enough of himself to get by, while protecting himself as much as possible.

I decided to display the kind of honesty I wanted from him. I said, "I have an idea of what's happening here. Would you like to hear it?" When he gave a non-committal answer, I repeated the question. Once I felt that he had really given me his consent, I said, "I think you don't like the story at all. I think you would like to get through this assignment without having to care about it. Is that right?"

The student looked surprised, then said, "Yeah, that's about it."

I responded, "In my class, you never have to do something you really don't want to do. You have a choice now. Would you like to be done with this story right now or find out how to make it something you like? Either way is OK with me. There is no grade riding on this either way."

The boy chose to stop right there. With his permission, I gave him a few final appreciations of his telling, then went on to another student.

Of course, I felt disappointed that he didn't trust me enough to involve himself in the story. But it was crucial that I honor his choice to do nothing. Only when he is safe from coercion will he be safe to care, to invest himself in a story. Until I make him really in charge, he will continue to direct his effort to holding me at a distance from which I can't hurt him. Eliciting and honoring his refusal to have a goal is the foundation of all future work we might undertake together.

EMOTIONAL BLOCKS

No one person can hope to meet all the emotional needs of fifteen or twenty (never mind thirty or forty!) children. Even though you lack the resources to meet all the needs, you can avoid the pitfall of ignoring their existence, of pretending that the cognitive realm is not influenced by the emotional realm.

Keep in mind that the most important "medicine" for emotional hurts (and also the most powerful tool of the coach) is listening. If a child comes to you upset, try listening. If a student starts to giggle or cry during a coaching session, keep listening. Do not assume that you must find a solution or console the student. Listening, free of judgment or attempts to control, is the single most helpful way to assist with emotional blocks.

The description of seventh-grader Brad's coaching session (pages 163-165) establishes another point about children and emotional blocks. The emotional healing process, like the physical healing process, often works more quickly (and the transition back from the healing mode is often more sudden) in children than in most adults.

FINDING THE KEY OBSTACLE

As the session with eighth-graders Olivia and Jennifer (page 191-193) exemplifies, you may not have time within a single class session both to establish the key obstacle and to help your student overcome it.

A great strength of the classroom teaching situation, however, is the opportunity to return to an obstacle another day—and another and another. You have the opportunity to fail many times and yet succeed brilliantly at last. Once your persistence has paid off, it will not matter how many attempts to help did not succeed, for your student will have overcome that particular obstacle, once and for all.

Students Becoming Coaches

When students learn to coach each other, they learn new advantages to working together. They gain a new sense of their own powers. And they learn to make better use of their own coaches.

Most students have no experience of the kind of coaching described here. They will need you to demonstrate it before they can learn it. Then, for their first attempts at being coaches, they will need a series of manageable tasks to try out. In time, they will be able to use more and more of the four-part structure with less and less supervision.

Demonstrate Coaching

Begin by coaching students, either in front of a group or privately. Your coaching may consist of one or more parts of the four-part structure—always beginning with listening, then optionally going on to appreciations, etc.

When you are ready to involve your class as active participants in the coaching process, explain briefly the first one or two parts of the four-part structure. Identify yourself as the coach, then expect them to assist you. You can start by having them coach a student volunteer. If you fear they will give hostile comments, however, start by having them coach you.

Let Them Coach You First

In a group that might have difficulty giving appreciations without digressing into suggestions or insults, begin by having the group coach you. Tell the group a story (or make a presentation of some other kind). Then say:

"I'd like you to coach me on my story. One way to coach me is to tell me what you liked about my story or about how I told it. Then I'll know what you liked, so I can do it even better next time.

"Raise your hand if you are willing to tell me something you think I did well, or that you liked about the story I told."

Call on a volunteer. If desired, coach him about his appreciation, saying something like,

- That was a wonderful appreciation. Thank you!
- So, you're saying it would have been better if more people had escaped. Does that mean you liked it when the old man escaped? (Student: Yes.) So, would your appreciation be that you liked the old man escaping?
- So, you're saying it would have been better if it had more gore in it. Was there anything about it you liked?
- What you just said seems like it was actually an insult. That doesn't help me get better at my storytelling. Is there anything about my story that you liked?
- Thank you for offering a suggestion, but now we are giving appreciations. Can you save that for another time?

LET THEM COACH ANOTHER STUDENT

When you think your class is ready to give appreciations to a student, ask for a volunteer to be coached. You might introduce the concept of coaching by saying something like this:

Some of you have been telling stories. There's a way of helping you get even better at storytelling, called "coaching." The first part of coaching is for us to listen very well to your story. The second part is to tell you what went well in your story.

Who would like to tell a story and let us coach you on it?

When a volunteer agrees to be coached, you might choose to establish immediately the principle that the teller is in charge:

Before you start your story, let me tell you that coaching is for you. You are in charge. Where would you like us to be? Where do you want to be?

When the teller takes charge of the physical environment, it helps the teller feel in charge. It may take such a concrete choice for the teller to understand what you mean by "in charge."

Once the student begins to tell, model excellent listening. If others do not follow your lead, remind them what you expect, emphasizing that their job is to help the student storyteller:

"Oops! This is coaching for Moy Fung. Right now, our job is to help her tell even better. Try to imagine the story she is telling."

After the story (if it seems to make sense to go on to appreciations) ask the student if she wants to hear what you liked about her story. Give an appreciation or two yourself. Ask the student,"Would you like to hear what other people liked about your story?"

If she agrees, say to the group, "To keep Moy Fung in charge, I think you should raise your hand. That way, Moy Fung can call on people when she is ready."

Call on volunteers to give appreciations to the student. Insist that they stick to giving appreciations! Forcefully interrupt any intentional insults. If volunteers seem confused about what appreciations are, explain again.

You can coach the group informally on their appreciations. When a group member gives an appropriate appreciation, for example, you can appreciate it, saying something like,

- What a great appreciation!
- You noticed something I didn't!
- Good noticing! The storyteller really created a sense that we were back with him in his old neighborhood.

You can even model asking permission, at the same time. Say to the group member whose appreciation you are coaching, "Can I tell you something I liked about your appreciation?"

If the group as a whole seems unable or unwilling to give appreciations, offer a few more appreciations of your own, then end the coaching session. Over the next days or weeks, model giving appreciations to several students; then try having the group give them once again. Consider letting them coach you once or twice; that way, you won't have to protect a volunteer storyteller at the same time that you teach the group how to give appreciations.

Another day, have the group help you coach another volunteer. Repeat regularly.

REDUCE YOUR INTERVENTION

Over time, your students will improve at listening and at giving appreciations. As your group becomes more adept at coaching, reduce your role to that of moderator. You can give fewer and fewer appreciations yourself, eliciting more and more from the group—until finally you say little more than, "Would you like to hear appreciations?" and later, "Can we stop appreciations now?"

One day, appoint a volunteer to be the "Moderator," "Dispatcher," or "Coach," who will ask the teller's permission to start and stop appreciations. The Coach can also have the job of making sure that the teller's needs remain the focus of the session.

If you wish, give the Coach the additional job of timekeeper. For example, you might agree in advance that you will devote no more than five minutes to appreciations. The Coach can announce, "We're almost out of time. Would you like one more appreciation?"

If a volunteer Coach is the moderator, you can still occasionally raise your hand to give appreciations or suggestions, just like any other member of the group.

BREAK INTO SMALL GROUPS

Once your group is skilled at listening to a single student, you can experiment with breaking into smaller groups for listening. Depending on your group and their experience with small-group work (and even on your physical facilities), it may be easier for them to break into pairs or into groups of four or five.

To break into pairs, you might say something like this:

"Do you remember how you coached each other by first listening very carefully to each other's stories? The most important part of coaching is that kind of listening. You've been doing it very well.

"I think you're ready to try it with a partner. In a minute, you'll get into pairs. One of you will be the talker, the other the Coach. The talker will just say anything you want for one minute. It doesn't even have to make much sense; this is just a chance for you to be listened to. The Coach will just listen delightedly. I'll tell you when to stop. Are you ready? Get a partner. One of each pair, raise your hand—you're the Coach. The other one will talk. Go!"

Adapt these directions as necessary. Your group may need you to specify who each person's partner is, or to briefly demonstrate with a volunteer partner in front of the group.

After one player has spoken for an entire minute, call "Time to stop!" If desired, ask some volunteers to answer the questions, "What was it like to listen for that long?" and "What was it like to talk that long?"

Have the pairs reverse their roles. Now the student who was the talker will be the Coach, and vice versa. Afterwards ask for comments, if desired.

Follow a similar procedure for groups of three, four or five—repeating the process until all have had a turn to speak.

Alternatively, divide into larger groups (such as groups of ten, or half the class), and have one person speak while all the others listen. In this format, don't expect each student to take a turn; one or two turns per group should be the maximum, especially at first.

Another day, repeat this entire exercise. When desired, specify that students should tell a story, or think aloud about an upcoming project. Increase the time period from one minute to an appropriate length of time.

One difficulty with coaching between students—like coaching between husband and wife—is that students have many roles with regard to each other. Students are also friends, playmates, sports competitors, and competitors for your attention.

To reduce confusion about overlapping roles, it may help to emphasize who is in the role of Coach at a given moment. It may help to have the Coach sit in a particular chair, or wear "the Coach's lanyard" or a special headband, or hold a particular physical object.

A LONG-TERM PROGRAM

For each part of the four-part structure, you can go through the following sequence to teach it to your students:

1. *Demonstrate individually and in groups.*
2. *Have the group coach you.*
3. *Have the group assist you in coaching a volunteer.*
4. *Have the group coach a volunteer without your intervention.*
5. *Have smaller groups coach each other.*

You can start teaching additional parts of the four-part structure before a group has completely learned a previous part. For example, when a group is at the fifth stage of learning to listen to each other, they will be listening to each other in small groups. At the same point in time, they may be only at the third stage of learning appreciations (assisting you in giving appreciations to a volunteer). All this may occur when you are just introducing them to the first stage of suggestions.

Depending on your group, you may introduce all four parts of the four-part structure in one week, or you may introduce a new part every two years!

It would not be unreasonable to spend all of first and second grade teaching students to listen and give appreciations, while you occasionally demonstrate suggestions. You might spend all of third grade helping students learn to give simple, positive suggestions; in fourth and fifth grade, you might have them explore questions as a form of suggestion.

An eighth-grade class, for another example, might spend a month or two learning appreciations, and then quickly go on to suggestions and "what else do you want from us?"

Some classes, on the other hand, even in the elementary grades, might learn the basics of all four parts in a single week. Then they might spend years learning to use the four-part structure more and more effectively.

Coaching across the Curriculum

Coaching is a useful structure for helping students learn any subject. The principles of coaching are applicable to any field of learning. The four-part structure can be adapted to almost any situation. The types of obstacles to your students' success are the same, no matter what subject they are learning.

As a result, you can coach your students on a wide variety of presentations. You can even coach their thought processes.

When you not only coach students but teach them to coach each other, you teach implicit lessons of cooperation and leadership. In the long term, you will find your classroom—and your role in it—transformed in gratifying ways.

WHAT TO COACH

"All right," you say. "I see how a storyteller tells a story, and the coach responds with the four-part coaching structure. But how do I use coaching in other subjects?"

Obviously, any oral presentation in the classroom can be coached, whether the presentation is storytelling, a book report, or a summary of a project. But the presentation need not even be oral. To coach a piece of writing, for example, the writing can be read aloud. (Have the writer choose who reads it: himself or another.) Or the coach can read the writing silently; in this case, the silent reading becomes the equivalent of listening to an oral presentation. A work of sculpture can be viewed, a machine manipulated, a non-working model examined.

Thus, a presentation of any kind—whether oral, written, recorded, crafted, or programmed into a computer—can be coached. But you need not save coaching until a presentation is prepared. Coaching can also help with the earlier stages of learning.

Language teachers are discovering the importance of "prewriting," the stage of thinking and discussing that can precede putting words on paper. Thinking aloud about a writing project can be helped by the coaching process. As always, the most helpful response is listening. Sometimes, the thinker-aloud will want to hear appreciations, too. Occasionally—infrequently, given the "baby" status of new projects—the student thinker will also want suggestions. Since the thoughts are new, the most helpful suggestions may take the form of questions that help the student gain more "experience of the subject"—questions that help the student imagine the subject more and find personal meanings in it.

Thinking aloud with a delighted listener (perhaps followed by appreciations and suggestions) can help any stage of learning. Imagine your students listening to each other as they respond aloud to your presentation about the causes of the American (U.S.) revolution, or the idea of light as waves, or the concept of a place-value system for numerical notation. Now imagine them learning to appreciate each other's thinking about these subjects. Imagine them making respectful suggestions to assist each other in making progress wherever they are stuck. You are imagining participatory, student-centered learning.

Coaching is a way of harnessing the power of another person's attention to help us learn. It puts that power within reach of your students in any stage of learning any subject.

COACHING OF THOUGHT PROCESSES

Most teachers have tools for evaluating students' access to facts and answers. Coaching also offers a tool for helping a student's thought processes.

For example, instead of just marking a student's incorrect math answer with an "X," you can coach the student about the problem at hand. Ask the student to describe his thinking about the problem. Don't listen only for what is "correct;" listen also to understand how he thinks about the problem. If the student is consistently reaching the same wrong answer, he must be consistently following the same "wrong" path in his thinking. By listening to him describe his thinking to you, you can come to understand what thinking he is doing well and what obstacle he faces. Only then can you give him the truly appropriate help.

I remember being a high school physics student. After failing the midterm exam, a classmate named Mike said to me, "I don't understand the teacher's answer to this question. How could speed be constant without adding more acceleration? When I drive a car, it slows down unless I keep my foot on the accelerator!"

Mike's statement to me revealed an obstacle to his learning physics. He had missed one of the main axioms of Newtonian physics: what we intuitively take to be the essential property of objects in motion (they soon come to rest unless something keeps moving them) is actually the result of two competing conditions (their essential property of continuing to move at the same speed and their being acted on by the forces of gravity and friction). Until Mike could catch on to this point, all the drills in the world would not teach him to calculate the correct answers to the questions on the physics exam.

If our teacher had known about coaching, he might have come to understand Mike's obstacle to learning physics. He might have listened to Mike explain how he arrived at his answer, and praised Mike's efforts to make sense of physics by comparing it to his own experience. He might have offered a suggestion to help Mike overcome his obstacle, perhaps by retracing Newton's thought processes in comparing the motion of celestial bodies to the motion of objects in daily life, or by helping Mike conduct a personal "experiment" with a near frictionless system (like a dry ice "hockey puck" on a smooth surface).

As it was, however, the class environment discouraged sharing our thought processes, especially if they might be "wrong." Our teacher never even knew why Mike was failing. Therefore, he was unable to help him succeed.

WHAT COACHING TEACHES

When students are coached, they learn specific content: they learn to tell stories, think about their writing, or clarify their thinking about a mathematics problem.

They also learn from the process of coaching, which teaches

about the helping process itself.

When you coach your students based on the assumption that they will succeed, they learn to expect success for themselves. They learn confidence.

Your students will also learn that obstacles are not defects, but temporary obstructions in a long-flowing river. They learn optimism.

Your students will also learn that they can be helped in a way that encourages their decision-making. They learn respect.

When a student sees you help other students, she learns, too—often more than she learns from her own coaching sessions. She compares and contrasts her struggles with those of the other students. Seeing their difficulties and paths to success, she learns about her own. While being a witness to another student's coaching, she is "off line," learning from the sidelines. She has a detachment that can add its own benefit.

A student may watch other students tackle obstacles that he may not yet be ready to tackle. He can watch the others succeed at something that he had not yet felt safe enough to attempt. Knowing now that success is possible, he may be more prepared to take the new risk.

Children have a natural desire to be helpful. Learning to coach helps them offer help in a constructive, respectful way. The four-part structure allows them to develop their helping abilities step-by-step.

When children learn to coach, they learn about teaching. Just as writing their own fiction helps fill the gap between being a book reader and a famous author, the four-part structure helps them fill the gap between being a student and an expert teacher.

Student coaches learn about leadership. They learn cooperation and teamwork. They learn to share in each other's triumphs.

SIGNS OF SUCCESS

When you coach students and help them learn to coach each other, you will find your classroom beginning to transform.

You will find your students learning more without your

intervention. They will take direction and information from you, but they will begin to use each other to assimilate your teaching. With the tools of mutual help in their hands, they will enjoy helping each other. Like toddlers gaining confidence, they may insist that you let them learn without you.

If your students were loud and disorganized, they may become quieter. But if they were obediently silent under your benign dictatorship, they may start buzzing with the heady process of democracy.

If your students were self-sufficient, they may start sharing more. If they were clingy, they may become bolder and more independent.

If they were grim, you may see them smiling more. If they were subserviently cheerful, you may see painful emotions arising, to be listened to, healed, and left behind as new moments demand new responses.

Your students will be more likely to share their ideas with you and with each other. In the beginning, this may seem more demanding of your time. In the long run, however, you will find yourself on a road that leads to their blossoming. By training your students to pay attention to each other, you make it possible for each one to get more of the attention she needs.

You will find your own role changing. You will become the resource person, the mentor. You will become the head coach and adviser of a team that is learning to help itself improve.

Taking Coaching to the World

Once you have learned what coaching is, you may want to know how to incorporate coaching into your life.

You may be thinking of how you'd like to be coached. You may also want to coach others. In either case, it usually makes sense to pursue both roles.

On the one hand, being coached well is the best preparation for coaching others. Once you've experienced supportive, incisive coaching, you will have firsthand knowledge of what you are trying to accomplish as a coach.

Conversely, learning to be a coach may help your own storytelling or other skill. Coaching others, at a minimum, can help you learn to make good use of coaches. Being a coach may also help you understand how to improve your own skills. Since it is often easier to think clearly about the improvements of others, assisting others may be the quickest route to understanding how to improve your own art. Finally, seeing others improve may help convince you that you can improve, too.

There are many relationships in which you can coach or be coached. You can hire a professional coach. You can establish a group devoted to coaching each other. You can also incorporate the principles and techniques of coaching into other relationships.

This chapter deals first with coaching partnerships, in which two of you come together to exchange coaching. Then, it suggests ways to incorporate coaching into other relationships.

Developing Coaching Partnerships

The simplest format for coaching is the coaching partnership, which consists of you and another person who agree to coach each other. Because of its simplicity and its availability, the coaching partnership is potentially the most powerful arena for coaching.

You may not be able to find a professional coach who suits you or be able to train your boss (or your spouse) to coach you well. But you can certainly find someone with whom you can form a successful coaching partnership.

WHO CAN BE A COACHING PARTNER?

The best person with whom to form a coaching partnership is someone you like and trust. Ask yourself, "Who would I like to spend more time with and become closer to? Who do I trust to be on my side and yet push me when I need pushing?"

The other person need not be a fellow storyteller or fellow corporate trainer. You may choose a performer in another art form, a teacher of other subjects, or just someone whose thinking and communication you respect.

It's not necessary that the other person wants to be coached on the same subject. The other person may want coaching on another kind of oral presentation, or even in an unrelated field.

Of course, another practitioner in your field can make an ideal coach. You share interest and familiarity with the field. The progress of either of you can directly inspire the other.

HOW TO APPROACH A POTENTIAL COACHING PARTNER

Once you have a potential coaching partner in mind, tell her briefly about coaching as you understand it. If you wish, give her a copy of this book and ask her opinion on it. Or invite her to watch a coaching video with you. (See page 2.)

Alternatively, offer to coach her. Set up a session in which you coach her, but she does not coach you. If you coach her well, she may want to have another session and be willing to learn to coach you in return.

State in your own words what you want from coaching, whether "I want someone who will listen to my stories and tell me what works in them," or "I'm looking for a partner to explore how to be really helpful with another artist."

Then suggest trying one session in which you take turns coaching each other. After the session, appreciate each other's coaching.

At this point, if you would like to meet again, say, "This was helpful for me. If you had your way, how often would we do this?" or "I'd like to do this once a month. How does that seem to you?" If your partner wants to meet weekly or monthly or once in a while, you have begun a new partnership. If not, you've learned that this person is no longer a candidate.

If you do not wish to meet again, say, "Thank you. I learned from this," but don't agree to meet again.

The Coaching Agreement

My coaching partner and I do not need to agree on anything else except to take turns coaching. We do not need to share goals, styles, audiences, or taste in stories. We do not even need to share art forms or types of projects. The less we need to agree on, the easier it is to retain clarity about the coaching agreement.

Therefore, the coaching agreement for each of us is some form of the following:

When I am the coach, I will devote the agreed-on time to helping you.

I will do my best to believe in your forthcoming success, to appreciate your current successes, to leave you in charge of your own goals, and to nurture your emotional safety.

I will free your attention from the clock by keeping track of the time allotted to helping you.

For this time period, your needs come first. If I am unable to put your needs first for any reason, I will advise you that I am unable to continue, and negotiate a change in plans.

When you are the coach, I will take responsibility for letting you know what kind of help I need at the moment.

Some implications of this agreement are discussed in the following sections.

TAKE TURNS

The essential agreement in a coaching partnership is to take turns. During a predefined time period, one of you is the coach while the other is the person being coached. During another time period, you reverse the roles.

This sounds simple but it is not always easy. You may each require gentle reminders about this unaccustomed concept of maintaining strict roles. In normal conversation, you shift back and forth frequently, discussing the concerns first of one of you, then of the other, then of the first again. In a coaching partnership, on the other hand, the only concerns to be discussed are those of the person being coached at the moment.

It may seem artificial or rigid to divide the two roles in this manner. But the behavior expected of the coach is demanding and very different from the behavior expected in other situations. You and your coaching partner are much more likely to end up mutually satisfied if you strictly observe the role division.

You can be very flexible, however, in deciding when to take each of these roles. For example, during one session you may each take one turn as coach. Or you may each take several shorter turns. Or one of you may be the coach this week, and the other next week.

Similarly, you can adapt your timing to your individual circumstances. If you do not live locally, for example, one of you may be able to benefit from being coached on the phone even if the other does not. In this case, you might coach one of you in weekly phone sessions and then coach the other in a longer monthly session, face to face.

KEEP YOUR COACHING RELATIONSHIP SEPARATE

The power of coaching stems from the coach's decision to put your interests first, for a specified duration. You and your coach cannot have a conflict of interests if your needs are guaranteed to come first.

The power of this clear role division will not be available if there is confusion about the coach's role. Unconscious confusion is especially apt to arise when you and your coaching partner have other roles with regard to each other—when you are also friends, colleagues, or mates.

I met my primary coaching partner, Jay, when I attended one of his weekend storytelling workshops. Over time, we became fellow board members of a storytelling organization, as well as friends. When we decided to try coaching each other, we realized that we needed to separate our coaching from our other relationships.

To make this separation clear, we divide our time into three parts. Before we begin coaching, we have a meal and talk as friends, catching up on each other's lives since our last meeting. This is our first time period. Then we agree how much total time we have remaining, and set an automatic timer for half of that time. In our second period, one of us takes a turn as coach for the other's stories, until the timer goes off. In the third time period, we set the timer again and reverse the roles. (If we have business to discuss, we add another period, agreeing to discuss it between our meal and our coaching, or else after our coaching is over.)

We also use changes in location to help us separate our multiple roles. We talk as friends at a restaurant, while taking a walk, or while sitting in a particular room. When we begin coaching, we move to another room. If we take a break between our two periods of coaching, we leave the "coaching room." Even after years of coaching together, we find that this physical move helps us maintain our agreed-upon roles.

When my wife and I exchange coaching time, we find it even more challenging to separate coaching from our other roles as confidants, lovers, roommates, financial partners, etc. We have the most success when only one of us gets coached on a particular day. We use a room chosen by the person being coached.

TAKE CHARGE OF GETTING WHAT YOU NEED

An advantage of coaching partnerships is the opportunity they offer to take control over getting and giving help. By training a helper, you escape the powerless feeling many of us had as children—when we could only accept or reject the helpers around us, but had no knowledge yet of how to "shape them up."

This means that it is beneficial for you to take charge of getting the kind of coaching you need. If your coach starts to criticize or inappropriately mixes suggestions with appreciations, you can ask for a change in your coach's behavior. You can say something like, "I have found that I do better when ...." Or, "Actually, right now it would help me to hear all of your appreciations before we get to suggestions." Or, "I can tell that you have some ideas for fixing this story, but right now I need to hear what you liked about it."

It is a lovely fantasy to expect perfect coaching without any effort on your part. But when you succeed at improving your partner's coaching, you gain in another way: not only do you receive better coaching, you establish for yourself that you have power over the quality of help that you get.

GETTING HELP WITH YOUR COACHING

The same basic principles and four-part structure that you use to coach others can also be used to help you improve your coaching.

If you and I are coaching partners, it might work for us to set aside part of a session just to coach one or both of us on our coaching. This session should include appreciations, perhaps followed by suggestions and whatever else we each desire. It can end with an appreciation or two.

HOW TO EVALUATE YOUR COACHING PARTNERSHIP

Even imperfect coaches have value. Anyone who can listen half-well can be of help to you. Imperfect coaches also give you a clear opportunity to practice training them.

Nonetheless, some partnerships are not worth pursuing. The effort and time required to make such a partnership succeed may be more than one of you is willing to invest. You may "push each other's emotional buttons" to an unacceptable degree. Or one of you may prove very slow to respond to the other's requests about coaching methods. Or the travel time or shortage of mutually available time slots may reduce the partnership's value to one or both of you.

So how do you decide which partnerships to stick with and which ones to work on? There is no single answer, but there are some factors to be sure to consider.

First, it is better to have a coach who listens to you (but is not competent to give appreciations or suggestions) than to have no coach at all.

Second, you don't have to settle for poor coaching. Make a conscious decision to use such coaching for its limited value, or to improve it, or else to replace it.

Third, what you think you need may be different from what you actually need.

When Jay and I had been meeting weekly for about two years, I grew dissatisfied. Struggling with the structure of a long story, I grumbled, "I coach Jay well on the structure of his stories. Why can't I get that kind of coaching from him?"

As my work on the story progressed, however, I realized that my need for help with structure was not my greatest need—exactly because I'm so good at it. Jay, on the other hand, has a great gift for noticing when a moment in a story has excitement to it. He seems to have an extra sense that responds to "sparks of life."

Jay's gift is invaluable to me in a coach, because it complements my own abilities. I may think I need help with structure (and from time to time I do), but I actually need more help with noticing which moments of a story come to life. Because I don't notice what Jay notices, I don't always notice his value to me. Until I realized what Jay had to offer, I didn't even know to ask for it.

Fourth, no one coach has to provide every advantage. In addition to my partnership with Jay, I have several other coaching partnerships that I call on occasionally when I need them. One coach is great for noticing rough edges on a mostly polished piece. Another has a gift for imagining what a rough piece could turn into. Another is very conscious of my movements on stage. Yet another has no tolerance for unnecessary words, and always helps me ferret them out. It's not important that Jay or anyone else be able to do *all* these things, only that I can find someone to give me the specific help I need at the moment.

In one way, coaching partnerships are like stories. I can tell a story well when I can determine what I love about it, what it means to me, or what I want to get out of it. In the same way, I can best decide about continuing a partnership when I am aware of the main advantage I get from it. Then I can compare the main thing I need at the moment with what I can get from the partnership.

If the partnership seems able to provide what I most need—at an acceptable cost in effort, time, and aggravation—then it is worth pursuing, at least until these factors change. If not, my efforts will be better spent pursuing other coaching relationships.

Learning from a Long-Term Partnership

A single session with an attentive coach can change your work forever. But a long-term coaching relationship can bring results of an even higher order.

In our years as coaching partners, Jay and I have been through conflicts, mistakes, and triumphs. Each new development seems to bring us closer and make more growth possible.

THE VALUE OF MISTAKES

No one enjoys the moment of learning about a major mistake. But the fruits of mistakes are worth pursuing.

After Jay and I had coached each other for about four years, he began to work on a story about his childhood friend nicknamed "Chickie." Since I usually approach new stories from the point of view of their structure, I suggested he do the same.

I led Jay through a series of sessions similar to those in "Needing More Experience of the Story" (pages 111-135). Over a period of months, we explored the themes—including social class and the value of family support—that Jay connected to his memories of his friend.

Some of Jay's memories were very powerful. He remembered the contrast between Chickie, whose father had left the family, and Jay, whose father was a comforting presence in Jay's life. Yet Jay's father was not only comfort, of course. To do justice to the theme of the father's role, Jay began exploring the dark side of his father's presence.

Every time we came up with another powerful scene that fit the story's theme, Jay spent days or weeks painstakingly weaving it into the fabric of the plot.

After eight months of work, "Chickie" had grown to nearly an hour in length. I was still hopeful about getting the themes to work themselves out, but Jay was discouraged both by his awareness that few individual scenes were working and by his sense that the story had grown unwieldy. He decided to drop the story indefinitely.

A short time later, Jay said to himself, "What if I went back to a simple story about Chickie, like the story I first envisioned?" Suddenly, the emotional "through-line" of the story (the core emotional progression) became clear to him, and the story began to "tell itself" in Jay's mind. When he told a few people this streamlined, thirty-five-minute version of the story, it seemed to work. After a few more trial performances with others, one day he confessed to me, "I decided to leave all that stuff out of the story." In short order, the story's true themes became clear to us both.

Months later, we were able to discuss what had happened. I had pushed him to fill out his conscious themes. But my pushing seemed to distance him from the handful of images that had first drawn him to his story. I had taken too active a role. I had also advocated a conceptual approach that only served to distract Jay from his story's core.

Only after a one-year detour on this major story did Jay and I come to understand how I needed to change my coaching to suit him.

Was this pleasant? No.

Was it helpful? Yes. It helped because we acknowledged the mistake, and learned from it. It helped because we stayed with it, even after this major difficulty in our coaching partnership.

THE VALUE OF PERSISTENCE

A year after finishing "Chickie," Jay came to me with his story, "Jeremy." (For a description of some of our work on that story, see "Guided-Fantasy Questions," page 132.)

It was clear to me that Jay had not yet found the essence of this story. I, of course, would have approached finding the essence by asking for statements from Jay.

But I had learned from our mistake with "Chickie" that Jay's road to a story's essence might lead through images rather than concepts. Further, I had noticed that much of the time wasted had been spent in patching the plot together each time Jay agreed to add a new scene.

What if I encouraged Jay to explore the images, without regard for thematic concepts? What if he could develop each new image without committing himself to integrating it seamlessly into the story?

I encouraged Jay to let the images lead the way, while keeping the plot fluid. I suggested that he imagine many scenes, then tell the ones that seemed most essential. After several such tellings, perhaps a plot would emerge of its own. After some resistance, Jay agreed to try "living freely but dangerously," as this approach felt to him.

Our new approach worked. "Jeremy" developed quickly and easily. Gone were my logical following of themes as well as Jay's painstaking, premature "sewing together" of the plot. In a few weeks, the story had transformed itself. Jay felt exhilarated, not exhausted.

At this point, we finally applied our earlier methods: checking that the themes were carried through and that the plot was appropriately tidy.

After the discouragement of a year working on "Chickie," Jay experienced the thrill of completely rewriting "Jeremy" in less than three months. If we had not made mistakes with "Chickie," learned from them, and continued to work together, we would not have experienced this success.

The next month, Jay was invited to create a new, full-evening show—with four months' notice. What story did Jay feel like creating? He wanted to create a story honoring his father, accurately reflecting the difficulties as well as the valuable support his father had been.

Realizing that our "failure" with "Chickie" had let Jay do the emotional groundwork for this new story—and encouraged by the quick, easy development of "Jeremy"—Jay agreed to this daunting schedule.

I said, "You will need many informal audiences for your rough drafts of this story. Why not ask groups of six or ten local storytellers to come listen to 'house concerts'?"

Jay said, "Do you really think people will come hear a story that's just taking shape?"

"I think they will," I replied. When Jay advertised to the local storytelling community, he was able to find more than twenty audiences. Some weeks, he told the story three times—each time with a different ending.

The result was Jay's ground-breaking story, "The Dance," which would never have come to be without our struggles to develop "Chickie." By trying, changing, and trying again, we had discovered how to work as a team to "fast-track" Jay's creativity.

THE VALUE OF FAILING IN MANY WAYS

After our triumphant success with "The Dance," we felt confident when Jay took on a "minor" story about his uncle, World War II hero Joseph T. O'Callahan.

Jay's uncle, known as "Father Joe," had been the chaplain aboard an aircraft carrier, the U.S.S. *Franklin*. When the *Franklin* was nearly sunk off the coast of Japan, Father Joe had organized groups of stunned sailors to save the ship.

After receiving the Congressional Medal of Honor, and without rest after two harrowing years on duty, Father Joe began a grueling, coast-to-coast fund-raising tour to sell war bonds. Midtour, he suffered a stroke. When he tried to return to his beloved career of teaching at a Jesuit college, he found himself physically unable to continue.

Years later, when Jay entered the Jesuit-run college as a freshman, he found his uncle helpful, sometimes irritating, completely unable to teach—but never bitter. He had in some way accepted his afflictions. At the time, young Jay had thought little of his uncle's attitude, but now it seemed an appealing part of the story.

The first problem in telling this story was whether to focus only on Father Joe's heroism in World War II. Jay created a striking way to tell the war story, using the grammatical second person: "Imagine that you are the carrier's captain. Standing on the bridge of your ship, you look down at the burning deck. Out of the smoke, you see a man running, identifiable only by the white cross on his helmet ...."

When Jay tried out the story of his uncle's heroics, he discovered that he didn't want to tell only a war story. There was something important in his personal experiences of Father Joe's later life that Jay wanted to include. This led to another problem: should Jay tell his personal experiences with his uncle before the war story, or after?

First, Jay tried telling the war story after the personal story. He told of the "gap" in his uncle's life: first, Father Joe was an athletic young man, then after the war, a "burnt-out shell." What had happened to cause this change? To answer this question, Jay told the battle scenes.

This first approach didn't work. The battle scenes didn't seem to really answer the question of how Father Joe had changed.

Next, Jay tried telling the battle scenes first. Then he could tell of the man he had known, and refer to the his uncle's experiences—even though, as a college freshman, young Jay had not known what his uncle had been through.

This second approach failed, too. The battle scene overpowered the personal story, which seemed like a lame anticlimax.

Obviously, the only other choice was to tell part of the personal story, then tell the battle story, then end with more of the personal story. After one unsatisfying performance, Jay set this version of the story aside, too.

A year later, Jay used a coaching session to return to this version of the story. As coach, I could listen with fresh ears after our hiatus.

Hearing the story again, I realized that it didn't work in its present form. If I had not already heard the other versions, I would have been tempted to recommend one of them as a solution. As it was, however, I realized that, of the three logical possibilities, none worked: the battle story could not be before the personal story, or after it, or in the middle of it!

If none worked, there had to be a different possibility. I believed in the story, and I believed in the possibility of Jay's success with it.

What possibilities had we overlooked? Jay had kept the battle story as a single block. What if Jay broke it up, and intercut sections of the battle story with sections of the personal story?

Jay seized upon this suggestion, saying, "This represents freedom over time!" Suddenly, he was free to tell snippets of the battle story as flashbacks from the personal story. He could tell some sections more than once. He could even tell parts of the battle story as flashforwards! He was free to juxtapose the two stories in a way that clarified their relationship.

This insight was the break-through in the development of this story, which was now clearly a "major" story in Jay's repertoire. This insight would not have been possible without our accumulated history of failures. We had to reach the point, like the chemist who discovered the structure of the benzene ring, where all the apparent possibilities did not work. Only then could we be forced into examining the unlikely but elegant solution.

UNEXPECTED BENEFITS

Over time, Jay and I have learned very specific ways to help each other efficiently. Obviously, you and your coaching partner will need different forms of help. Your job is not to help each other just as Jay and I do, but to grow in your own ways.

I can't predict what you will learn from your relationship with your coaching partner, but I can predict that it will continue to change.

You might think that, as time goes on, Jay and I would need less time giving appreciations. In fact, we have found that appreciations have become ever more powerful between us. Since appreciations accomplish more, we actually spend less time giving suggestions.

Recently, through suggestions, I helped Jay notice an emotional block in his latest story. I could notice the block because I know him so well. When I helped him identify and overcome his block, he had a new comprehension of my unique knowledge of him and dedication to improving his work.

I, in turn, felt Jay's gratitude for my coaching over our long relationship. I knew more deeply than ever that we were allies in the creative process.

Now, when I appreciate specific lines in one of his new stories, Jay receives these appreciations in a new way. Each appreciation seems to have the power of our whole relationship behind it, of my whole comprehension of Jay's abilities, struggles, and potential. Jay seems to understand more quickly what I see in his story, and thus be able to improve the rest of it without the need for detailed suggestions from me.

We seem to have returned to the basic principle of giving appreciations, but from a new vantage. Who knows what is next for us? Who knows what is next for you and your coaching partner, either!

Coaching as a Form of Leadership

Once you have experienced the principles of coaching in action, you may start asking, "Why can't some of my other relationships be based on the same principles?"

There is no reason why they can't.

As a storyteller (or bicyclist, product designer, or sales person) and as a coach, you must adapt these principles and techniques in a way that makes sense for you. While you're at it, you can adapt them in a way that makes sense for your job, your family, and your neighborhood.

You can use coaching in business, in social services, in education, and in creative work of all kinds, as well as in the performing arts.

SUPERVISION MADE SUPPORTIVE

You can make your own adaptation of coaching and then apply it to any supervisory relationship in your job or voluntary organizations.

If you supervise staff, ask their permission before giving comments. Give them appreciations ... often. Give them suggestions ... thoughtfully. Ask them how else you can be of help to them.

If you are supervised by someone else, try teaching her about coaching by first coaching her well. Listen to her. Offer appreciations freely. If there is little to appreciate, offer the same appreciations often. After twenty or thirty appreciations, ask if she wants to hear a suggestion. Make the first suggestion a minor one. If she comes anywhere close to heeding it, praise her thoroughly.

After several weeks or more of this campaign, offer a suggestion: "Do you want to hear something that would help me? It would help me improve, I think, if you let me know what I'm doing well before you made your suggestions. I think I could hear better what you have to say."

Little by little, help your supervisor learn what you need. It will help both of you, and your organization as well.

WATCH FOR ROLE CONFLICTS

As you introduce coaching into other relationships, be aware of overlapping roles that have conflicting expectations.

Be especially aware of any "gatekeeper" roles—roles which require evaluation. For example, the supervisor who makes a decision about promotion is presumably acting as gatekeeper, preventing unqualified applicants from entering the higher job rung. For another example, think of a festival producer who must decide which storytellers to hire. He is a gatekeeper who must make sure that the chosen tellers meet the needs of the festival.

All such gatekeeper roles are in direct conflict with the role of coach. The coach tries to see your potential and move you closer to it, whereas the gatekeeper must make a realistic evaluation of your current achievements.

One person can act in both roles—but not at the same moment. If I understand that I am called upon to perform two conflicting roles, I can at least separate them conceptually. I can say, "As your coach, I see that you are developing a new approach to combining storytelling and comedy that has the potential to contribute something unique to both art forms. I look forward to enjoying those contributions. As the producer of this radio show, I need something that is fully polished right now."

Another situation that requires clarity about roles is encountered in "story sharing groups," in which storytellers come together to tell stories in a supportive atmosphere. Some expect a performance, albeit an informal one. A performance happens for the sake of the audience. Others expect the listeners to be coaches, which means that the event is held for the sake of the storytellers. Either arrangement is fine, but the participants will only be satisfied if they agree whether the storyteller is acting as the provider of services or as the person being served.

A FORM OF LEADERSHIP

Leadership consists of taking responsibility for the success of an entire enterprise. It follows that many people can be leaders in the same group, all at the same time. In fact, the more who are taking leadership, the better the group will do. This true form of leadership is not competitive, but cooperative. It is not based on conquest, but on connection.

Storytelling, like all creative arts, is potentially a form of leadership that uses the imagination to suggest what we can become.

Coaching is potentially a form of leadership that uses carefully delineated helping relationships to help us become what we can imagine.

This leadership does not need a mass movement; it can be practiced in a group of two. By demonstrating that you and I can assist each other, we become allies in our creativity and empowerment. We experience that we are each capable of success, and that, in spite of any commercial messages to the contrary, we need each other more than we need anything else.

Each successful coaching relationship, furthermore, is a potential source of hundreds of other such relationships. After all, once you and I have constructed one successful, supportive relationship, we will not easily settle for less in our other relationships. Others will start to notice, too, how much fun we're having and how well we're doing. They'll want to learn how to do the same.

There may be shortages of many material goods. But there is no shortage of people. Once we learn how to train each other to help, there will be no shortage of effective help. Imagine such a life! Imagine such a world!

Our society perpetuates the great, destructive fallacy that we must always "go it alone." Coaching, on the other hand, is a technique for harnessing the awesome power of "going it together." It helps us taste the delicious joy of living a fully supported life. It helps us experience the productive power of giving—and expecting—effective help in bringing out each others' potential.

SOURCES

This chapter gives my sources for the stories and coaching sessions that appear in the text.

For each *story*, there is a description of my source. If I adapted a traditional tale, I give my first source plus one or two others I have consulted, as well as a summary of the changes I have made.

For each *coaching session*, there is a description of how fictionalized the session is, the name of the storyteller (if I know it and the storyteller wants it known), and where to reach the storyteller. Unless noted as a pseudonym, the teller's actual first name is used.

I'd love to receive any corrections or omissions to these notes—especially if I coached you but have lost track of how to reach you.

The book by Bruno Bettelheim mentioned in the introduction is, of course, *The Uses of Enchantment: The Meaning and Importance of Fairy Tales* (New York: Vintage Books, 1977).

The National Storytelling Festival (mentioned in the Introduction) continues to thrive and grow. For more information about this and other storytelling events, courses, and local organizations, contact the National Storytelling Association, P.O. Box 309, Jonesborough, Tennessee, 37659 (800-525-4514).

People sometimes ask me where I learned to coach. Mostly, of course, I learned by doing. Several of the concepts and structures in this book, however, are adapted from Re-evaluation Counseling (Co-Counseling), which is a process in which two or more people exchange help with each other in order to free themselves from the effects of past hurtful experiences. The principles of coaching that I describe are similar to some of the guiding principles used in Re-evaluation Counseling (R.C.). My four-part structure and my "coaching agreement" are my own elaboration of formats used in R.C. My thoughts about leadership, the emotional healing process, and the importance of supportive relationships are derived in part from R.C. theory. For information about books, recordings, classes, and existing networks of Co-Counselors, write: Rational Island Press, 719 2nd Avenue North, Seattle, Washington, 98109.

COACHING PRINCIPLES 29

ZUSIA

I first heard this told by the late Reuven Gold of Chicago. It is widely known among Jews in the United States. I have retold it in my own words. A version appears in *Tales of the Hasidim: Early Masters*, Martin Buber (New York: Schocken Books, 1947, page 251). Many other versions can be found, including these: *Hasidism: The Movement and Its Masters*, Harry M. Rabinowicz (Northvale, NJ: Jason Aronson, Inc., 1988, page 107); and *A Touch of Wisdom, A Touch of Wit*, Shmuel Himelstein (Brooklyn, NY: Mesorah Publications, 1991, page 61).

LESSON FROM A MASTER

From the book *Cellist* by Gregor Piatigorsky. Copyright ©1965 by Gregor Piatigorsky. Reprinted by permission of Doubleday, a division of Bantam Doubleday Dell Publishing Group, Inc.

THE MOMENT THE MASTERPIECE WAS CREATED

I adapted and rewrote this story from a traditional Zen tale that I first read in *Zen Flesh, Zen Bones*, Paul Reps (Garden City, NY: Doubleday Anchor Books, 1961, page 23).

A STRUCTURE FOR COACHING 47

The section on listening was inspired in part by Brenda Ueland's article, "Tell Me More" in *Strength to Your Sword Arm: Selected Writings* (Duluth, Minnesota: Holy Cow Press, 1993).

RISING ABOVE IT

This is my reinterpretation of a traditional Zen story. I first came across the tale in *The Wisdom of the Zen Masters*, Irmgard Schloegl (New York: New Directions, 1976, page 21).

ELLIOT COLEMAN'S GIFT

This is how it happened to me in Baltimore in 1966-67.

A WORD AND A SENTENCE

Mischa Borodkin was my father-in-law for fourteen years. He was my second father, and a great supporter of my early adulthood. This is my version of one of the many stories Mischa told of his long and inspiring career.

THE TEACHER'S RESTRAINT

This is a true story from my personal experience as a student at Niles Township Community High School, West Division, Skokie, Illinois.

THE FAMOUS STORY I WILL NEVER READ

This is my recollection of incidents from my masters program at Hollins College, Roanoke, Virginia. George Garrett is the author of many novels and volumes of short stories.

JERRY

This is a fictionalized coaching session. The interaction between coach and storyteller are based on several coaching sessions with various storytellers; the search for a new ending to the "China Doll" story is taken from my own work. My finished version of the story can be heard on audiocassette: *Keep On Shaking: A Gentle Wind,* Doug Lipman (Enchanters Press, P.O. Box 441195, W. Somerville, Massachusetts, 02144, 617-391-3672.)

Coaching to Overcome the First Obstacle: Lack of Information 89

EILEEN

The actual session with Eileen can be viewed on videotape: *Coaching Storytellers: a Demonstration Workshop for All Who Use Oral Communication*, Doug Lipman (Enchanters Press, 1993. VHS videotape. P.O. Box 441195, W. Somerville, Massachusetts, 02144, 617-391-3672).

Eileen Curran can be reached at 155 Ames St., Sharon, Massachusetts, 02067.

NATALIE

This session—based on an actual session in which I coached professional storyteller Connie Dodge about creating songs—has been fictionalized substantially.

THE TEACHER'S ANGER

This is a true story. I spent much of my academic year asking Lenci questions about how she would deal with various problems of teaching. My debt to her is enormous.

The successor to the Kodály Musical Training Institute, in a new location and with new staff, still gives outstanding training. It can be reached at Kodály Institute at Capitol, Conservatory of Music, Capitol University, Columbus, Ohio, 43209-2394.

JASON

This session is not based on my work with any actual storyteller. I created a fictitious teller who would require many forms of explanation before understanding what I meant.

AUDREY

I have explained this basic framework to many storytellers. "Audrey" is fictitious.

THE GIANT IN THE SKY

I heard Jean Piaget's actual experience described in a course I took at Wheelock College in the mid-1970s. Over the years, I have told it to many workshops, unconsciously changing it in the process. I have been unable to locate a printed version of the incident.

THE THREE GUIDES

This original story was inspired by a Sufi tale about a man who seeks a lamp because it will help him read at night, not realizing that he must already know how to read in the daytime. The Sufi story was created by Shaikh-Pir Shattari, who died in India in 1632. I found the story and the information about its author in *Tales of the Dervishes,* Idries Shah (New York, E.P. Dutton, 1970).

COACHING TO OVERCOME THE SECOND OBSTACLE: NEEDING MORE EXPERIENCE OF THE STORY 111

GUY

The actual session with Guy can be viewed on videotape: *Coaching Storytellers: a Demonstration Workshop for All Who Use Oral Communication,* Doug Lipman (Enchanters Press, 1993. VHS videotape).

Guy Peartree is a professional African-American storyteller who can be reached at 4 Hubbard St., Jamaica Plain, Massachusetts, 02130.

BETTY

Betty's session is transcribed from an audiotape. The actual ending of her story depended on gestures; I fictionalized it and the corresponding parts of her session to make it work in print. Years after taping this coaching session, I am not actually sure of Betty's identity.

AMY

Amy's session was videotaped. I edited it substantially, for clarity.

Amy Tighe can be reached at P.O. Box 1914, Harvard Square, Cambridge, Massachusetts, 02238.

NED

The first half of Ned's session is transcribed from an audiotape. Years after taping this coaching session, I am not actually sure of "Ned's" identity. The second half is fictionalized, based on several remembered sessions with other tellers.

DEREK

The actual session with Derek can be viewed on videotape: *Coaching Storytellers: a Demonstration Workshop for All Who Use Oral Communication,* Doug Lipman (Enchanters Press, 1993. VHS videotape).

Derek Burrows can be reached at 2 Glenvale Terrace, Jamaica Plain, Massachusetts, 02130.

WINONA

Winona's session is transcribed from an audiotape and edited for brevity and clarity. The storyteller's actual first name is Robbi.

JAY

Jay's session was reconstructed from memory, as accurately as possible.

Jay O'Callahan can be reached at P.O. Box 1054, Marshfield, Massachusetts, 02050.

Jay's recording of *Jeremy: A Christmas Story* is available from Artana Recordings at the same address.

At this writing, the chapter-book version of Jeremy is in preparation by Peachtree Publishers, 494 Armour Circle N.E., Atlanta, Georgia, 30324, 800-241-0113.

COACHING TO OVERCOME THE THIRD OBSTACLE: MISDIRECTED EFFORT 137

MY EVIL LANDOWNER

This session is recalled from memory, as accurately as possible. (In the story, the actual character is not the landowner but the steward of the estate, who is acting for the landowner.)

The finished story, "Pulling the Thorn," can be heard on audiotape: *The Forgotten Story: Tales of Wise Jewish Men,* Doug Lipman (Yellow Moon Press. P.O. Box 1316, Cambridge, Massachusetts, 02238, 800-497-4385).

My coach was Jay O'Callahan.

BRENDA

The actual session with Brenda can be viewed on videotape: *Coaching Storytellers: a Demonstration Workshop for All Who Use Oral Communication,* Doug Lipman (Enchanters Press, 1993. VHS videotape).

Brenda Chiavarini is an actress and storyteller and can be reached at 1532 Brockton Ave. #5, Los Angeles, California, 90025.

JUNE

June Barr's session is transcribed from an audiotape. The dialogue on page 104 is fictional, created to give the essence of what happened quickly and elliptically in the actual session.

PAULINE

Pauline's session is transcribed from an audiotape and edited for brevity and clarity. Pauline is a pseudonym.

ABBY

Abby's session is transcribed from an audiotape. Much of the actual session was nonverbal. I have added dialogue to convey the feeling of what actually happened. Years after taping this coaching session, I am not sure of "Abby's" identity.

COVERING THE MOON ON HER FOREHEAD

This is another original story that was inspired by a Sufi story. The motif of the woman with a moon (or star) on her forehead appears in several folktales. See motif F545.2 Remarkable forehead; for an African story with this motif, see *Folktales of Strong Women,* Doug Lipman (Yellow Moon Press. P.O. Box 1316, Cambridge, Massachusetts, 02238, 800-497-4385.) The Sufi story (about a man who is obsessed with his beard) appears in the thirteenth century Parliament of the Birds; I first saw it in Idries Shah, *Caravan of Dreams* (London: Octagon Press. 1988).

JAY

Jay's session was reconstructed from memory, as accurately as possible.

Jay O'Callahan can be reached at P.O. Box 1054, Marshfield, Massachusetts, 02050.

GORDON

I have coached many people the way I describe in this fictitious session. Reading the following book, I first learned of the technique of asking people to do purposely what they habitually try to avoid: *A Soprano on Her Head*, Eloise Ristad (Moab, UT: Real People Press, 1982).

BOY SEEKS DOG

I created this story to illustrate the point about misdirected effort. I had been reading book after book of Sufi stories, so I'm sure they exerted a major influence.

RHONDA

I have coached many people the way I describe in this fictitious session.

COACHING TO OVERCOME THE FOURTH OBSTACLE: EMOTIONAL BLOCKS 157

For a clear, more detailed explanation of the emotional healing process (in the context of listening skills for parents), see the series of booklets and audiocassettes by Patty Wipfler (Parents Leadership Institute, P.O. Box 50492, Palo Alto, California, 94303).

DORIS

Doris told this story during a coaching session at a conference. I do not know her actual name or where to reach her. (If you read this, "Doris," please call or write!) I transcribed the session from memory, after years had elapsed.

MY "JACK AND THE BULL"

I transcribed this session from memory, after several years. My coach was Lee-Ellen Marvin, who can be reached at ***.

BRAD

I transcribed this session from memory, after several years. "Brad" is a pseudonym.

GAIL

This is another session that I reconstructed, years later.

Gail Rosen is a professional performer who describes herself as a "Jewish, Feminist, Inspirational" storyteller. She can be reached at 721 Howard Rd., Pikesville, Maryland, 21208.

REBECCA

I transcribed this session from a videotape; it was edited for clarity and brevity. Then, in response to the teller's wishes, I created a new story rather than include excerpts from her original story. "Rebecca" is a pseudonym.

NEIL

When listening to an audiotape of an old coaching workshop, I heard myself telling about Neil—who's "progress report" I had long since forgotten. I'm not even sure of the actual identity of the original "Neil."

GEORGINA

Georgina told her story at a workshop. I'm not sure of her actual name, nor of the author of the story she told. Please contact me if you know either person's name.

FINDING THE KEY OBSTACLE 177

BARBARA

Several years after this session, I described it from memory. Barbara is a storyteller from Cleveland, Ohio.

STEVE

The actual session with Steve can be viewed on videotape: *Coaching Storytellers: a Demonstration Workshop for All Who Use Oral Communication*, Doug Lipman (Enchanters Press, 1993. VHS videotape).

Steve Rosenthal describes his storytelling this way: "I draw on my varied background as a business executive, sailor, and parent. I also run a Business of Storytelling workshop." He can be reached at 12 Mark St., Natick, Massachusetts, 01760.

CARLA

I wrote this session from memory, after several years. "Carla" is a pseudonym.

OLIVIA AND JENNIFER

This session was videotaped informally—but the tape is crude enough that it's not always clear what happens. I reconstructed the ending in a way that illustrates my experience with students who faced similar obstacles. The names are pseudonyms.

A LIFETIME SUPPLY

I based this story on one given in *Tales of the City of God,* Carlos G. Valles (Chicago: Loyola University Press, 1993, page 92); Valles's collection of "parables from all times and cultures" gives no source. In his version, a pregnant woman is asked by a spiritual master to imagine how much rice her unborn child would eat in a lifetime.

COACHING IN THE CLASSROOM 195

MISDIRECTED EFFORT

In this section, I describe a coaching session with a high school student who was known as "bright troublemaker." I reconstructed his coaching session from memory.

TAKING COACHING TO THE WORLD 223

JAY (SEVERAL SESSIONS FROM PAGE 178 TO PAGE 192)

The stories by Jay O'Callahan described here can be heard on audiotapes available from Artana Records, P.O. Box 1054, Marshfield, Massachusetts, 02050, 800-626-5356:

"Chickie, Coming Home to Someplace New."

"The Dance."

"Father Joe: A Hero's Journey."

Other Books from August House Publishers

Through a Ruby Window

A Martha's Vineyard Childhood

Susan Klein

Hardback $19.95 / ISBN 0-87483-416-3

The Farm on Nippersink Creek

Stories from a Midwestern Childhood

Jim May

Paperback $18.95 / ISBN 0-87483-339-6

Once upon a Galaxy

The ancient stories that inspired Star Wars, Superman, and other popular fantasies

Josepha Sherman

Hardback $19.95 / ISBN 0-87483-386-8

Paperback $11.95 / ISBN 0-87483-387-6

The Storyteller's Start-Up Book

Finding, Learning, Performing, and Using Folktales

Margaret Read MacDonald

Hardback $23.95 / ISBN 0-87483-304-3

Paperback $13.95 / ISBN 0-87483-305-1

Queen of the Cold-Blooded Tales

Roberta Simpson Brown

Paperback $9.95 / ISBN 0-87483-408-2

Race with Buffalo

and Other Native American Stories for Young Readers

Collected by Richard and Judy Dockrey Young

Hardback $19.95 / ISBN 0-87483-343-4

Paperback $9.95 / ISBN 0-87483-342-6

AUGUST HOUSE PUBLISHERS, INC.

P.O. BOX 3223

LITTLE ROCK, AR 72203

1-800-284-8784